T0328610

Cambridge Elements ≡

Elements in Forensic Linguistics
edited by
Tim Grant
Aston University
Tammy Gales
Hofstra University

FORENSIC LINGUISTICS IN CHINA

Origins, Progress, and Prospects

Yuan Chuanyou
Guangdong University of Foreign Studies
Xu Youping
Guangdong University of Foreign Studies
Lu Nan
Guangdong University of Foreign Studies

CAMBRIDGE
UNIVERSITY PRESS

Shaftesbury Road, Cambridge CB2 8EA, United Kingdom

One Liberty Plaza, 20th Floor, New York, NY 10006, USA

477 Williamstown Road, Port Melbourne, VIC 3207, Australia

314–321, 3rd Floor, Plot 3, Splendor Forum, Jasola District Centre, New Delhi – 110025, India

103 Penang Road, #05–06/07, Visioncrest Commercial, Singapore 238467

Cambridge University Press is part of Cambridge University Press & Assessment, a department of the University of Cambridge.

We share the University's mission to contribute to society through the pursuit of education, learning and research at the highest international levels of excellence.

www.cambridge.org
Information on this title: www.cambridge.org/9781009478533

DOI: 10.1017/9781009162548

First published 2024

A catalogue record for this publication is available from the British Library.

ISBN 978-1-009-47853-3 Hardback
ISBN 978-1-009-16253-1 Paperback
ISSN 2634-7334 (online)
ISSN 2634-7326 (print)

Forensic Linguistics in China

Origins, Progress, and Prospects

Elements in Forensic Linguistics

DOI: 10.1017/9781009162548
First published online: April 2024

Yuan Chuanyou
Guangdong University of Foreign Studies

Xu Youping
Guangdong University of Foreign Studies

Lu Nan
Guangdong University of Foreign Studies

Author for correspondence: Yuan Chuanyou, richyuan@163.com

Abstract: This Element offers a comprehensive examination of forensic linguistics in China. It traces the origins of the field in the 1980s and 1990s, and highlights the progress made in the 2000s, with a focus on the work of influential scholars such as Pan Qingyun, Wang Jie, Du Jinbang, Liao Meizhen, Yuan Chuanyou, and Wang Zhenhua. It discusses the development of Discourse Information Theory, the Principle of Goal, Functional Forensic Discourse Analysis, and Legal Discourse as a Social Process. It also analyses studies on language evidence and explores legal translation. It discusses emerging research areas, including cyberbullying language research, internet court discourse analysis, authorship analysis, expert assistance systems, and speaker identification and evidence of forensic phonetics. This Element provides valuable insights into the growth and potential of forensic linguistics in China, serving as a comprehensive resource for scholars, researchers, and practitioners interested in the intersection of language and law.

Keywords: Forensic linguistics in China, legal linguistics, origins, progress, prospects

ISBNs: 9781009478533 (HB), 9781009162531 (PB), 9781009162548 (OC)
ISSNs: 2634-7334 (online), 2634-7326 (print)

Contents

Series Preface

The Elements in Forensic Linguistics series from Cambridge University Press publishes across four main topic areas: (1) investigative and forensic text analysis; (2) the study of spoken linguistic practices in legal contexts; (3) the linguistic analysis of written legal texts; and (4) explorations of the origins, development, and scope of the field in various countries and regions. *Forensic Linguistics in China: Origins, Progress, and Prospects* by Yuan Chuanyou, Xu Youping, and Lu Nan provides our third Element in this latter area following on from Elements exploring the nature and contribution of forensic linguistics in the Philippines and Australia.

All three authors of *Forensic Linguistics in China* have been significant contributors to the discipline in their country, and are increasingly known internationally. Yuan Chuanyou has not only contributed significant research in the field but has also been a member of the Executive Committee of the organisation (now known as) the International Association of Forensic and Legal Linguistics, and in this role was instrumental in bringing the 12th Biennial Conference of *The International Association for Forensic and Legal Linguistics* to Guangzhou, China in 2015. Xu Youping has long worked in the field, and as set out in this Element, has recently turned to the problem of cyberbullying and online abuse, and how forensics linguistics can assist in tackling this global problem. To those outside of China, Lu Nan is less well known, but his work on legal argument helps exemplify the breadth of work currently being pursued within Chinese forensic linguistics. In this Element, we see the broad range of not only their contributions but the theoretical and practical projects of other Chinese forensic linguists including Professors Du Jinbang and Liao Meizhen.

As the subseries of *Origins* Elements progresses, one fascinating theme that is brought to the fore is the definition of the discipline, and this Element contains an explicit discussion of the term 'Forensic Linguistics' and its varying translations into Mandarin Chinese and the different connotations of the different translations. This definitional question naturally intersects with the conception of the scope of the discipline, which as readers will discover starts with the legal interests of language and law studies but has gradually spread to the more investigative domains, although we are yet to see much use of forensic linguistics in Chinese courts.

Overall, this is a valuable contribution to the Elements series both itself by providing a fascinating insight into Chinese forensic linguistics, and also in terms of contrasts with other countries and jurisdictions already covered in the growing *Origins* subseries. We look forward to more of the same.

Tim Grant
Series Editor

1 Introduction

Forensic linguistics, along with the renaming of its affiliated international association (from *The International Association for Forensic Linguists* (IAFL) to *The International Association for Forensic and Legal Linguistics* (IAFLL)) in 2021 (see Section 4.1), now falls under the umbrella of Legal and Forensic Linguistics. This encompasses two distinct but complementary areas of research and practice in the field of language and law: legal linguistics and forensic linguistics.

Legal linguistics focuses on the analysis of written and spoken language used in legal contexts, examining the language employed by judges, lawyers, mediators, arbitrators, and police officers. It encompasses the study of legal language in a broad sense, exploring linguistic features, rhetorical strategies, and ontological aspects of legal language. This branch of research aims to understand and analyse legal texts such as legislation, contracts, and court decisions, shedding light on the language used in the legal domain. Forensic linguistics, on the other hand, delves into how language-related issues are addressed within the legal system. It specifically deals with language evidence, encompassing the research and practice of language *as* evidence, language *in* evidence, and the language *of* evidence. In common law jurisdictions, forensic linguistics often focuses on the analysis of language used in legal disputes, such as authorship attribution, discourse analysis, and linguistic profiling.

In the Chinese context, forensic linguistics is influenced by the civil law system. As a result, it originally emphasised the 'legal' side rather than the 'forensic' side. Chinese forensic linguistics focuses on the linguistic analysis of legal language, including legislative texts, court proceedings, and legal documents. It explores how language is used and understood within the legal framework in China.

This Element provides a comprehensive exploration of the field of forensic linguistics in China. It traces the origins of forensic linguistics in the 1980s and 1990s up until the progress made in the 2000s, and then discusses the prospects for Legal and Forensic Linguistics in China. Areas covered include legal language studies by Chinese language scholars and forensic linguistics by foreign language scholars, highlighting the contributions of scholars like Pan Qingyun and Wang Jie, and the work of Du Jinbang on Discourse Information Theory (DIT), Liao Meizhen on the Principle of Goal, Yuan Chuanyou on the Functional Forensic Discourse Analysis, and Wang Zhenhua on the explorations of Legal Discourse as a Social Process.

1.1 Legal Linguistics: The Study of Legal Language

The concept of the 'language of the law' or 'legal language' refers to the language used by lawyers and legal professionals, particularly in common law jurisdictions where English is the official language (Mellinkoff, 1963). This language is characterised by several features, as identified by Mellinkoff and later discussed by Tiersma.

Mellinkoff (1963: 3) identifies nine characteristics of the language of the law: frequent use of common words with uncommon meanings; frequent use of Old English and Middle English words; frequent use of Latin words and phrases; use of Old French and Anglo-Norman words not commonly used; use of terms of art; use of argot; frequent use of formal words; deliberate use of words and expressions with flexible meanings; and attempts at extreme precision of expression.

Tiersma (2005), while acknowledging these characteristics, challenges some of the common misconceptions about legal language. He argues against the notion that legal language is archaic and conservative, providing examples to demonstrate that archaic language is not as prevalent as it used to be (Tiersma, 2005: 6). He also counters other myths, such as legal language being wordy and redundant, pompous and dull, and precise. Tiersma concludes that the idea of legal language as a monolithic entity is a myth (Yuan et al., 2018).

Renowned legal scholar Professor Su Li (Zhu) shares similar views on legal language, specifically legal Chinese. Su Li (2023: 91) argues that legal language is not inherently precise and accurate, as its precision and ambiguity depend on the interests of the parties involved. He also highlights that the meaning of legal words can change with social interests and situations. Su Li criticises the use of complex and unnecessary language, referring to it as a form of professional decoration (Su Li, 2023: 100), echoing the concepts of Mellinkoff's 'professional monopoly' and Tiersma's 'aura of erudition to one's writing'. He agrees with Judge Posner's criticism of American legal professionals who use Latin words instead of plain English, and he critiques Chinese law professors who adopt American legalese, such as *chilling effect* and *prima facie validity*. Su Li emphasises the importance of clear communication and suggests that professionals who cannot speak clearly may be on the wrong track, even with extensive knowledge (Su Li, 2023: 101).

While some ideas in the article are accepted by the legal linguistic community, there are criticisms. Some scholars dispute the claim that there is no legal language, arguing that studying legal and judicial language is necessary. The article's use of 'legal language', 'legal words', 'legal terminology', and 'legalese' interchangeably lacks consistency and may lead to misunderstandings. Su Li's statement that there may be an abstract legal language, but it should not be taken seriously, is controversial. Even the founding father of Chinese legal linguistics, Mr Pan Qingyun, lamented, 'Is the existence of legal language questionable? There is no doubt that "legal language" does exist. As for the existence or non-existence of "legal or forensic linguistics", people do not see eye to eye. I do not see the need to force a uniform definition. In order to avoid entanglement, I call it "legal language studies"' (WeChat discussion). Pan's work will be elaborated in Sections 2 and 3.

It is natural for legal scholars and legal linguists to have different perspectives and reasons for their focus on language issues, which can lead to clashes in views. Professor Janet Ainsworth, past president of the IAFL, has called for interdisciplinary exchange and sharing among colleagues in the academy. She urges forensic linguists to take the first step in promoting interdisciplinarity by publishing their papers in law journals (Ainsworth, 2020).

1.2 Forensic Linguistics: The Study of Language Evidence in China

As the titles or subtitles of the seminal works on forensic linguistics (Shuy, 1993; Eades, 1995, 1998; Coulthard & Johnson, 2007; Liu, 2009; Coulthard et al., 2017) suggest, this discipline studies language evidence or language in evidence or language as evidence in legal settings, particularly in the courtroom. Clearly, language evidence has been the most important focus since the discipline's inception. However, it is notable that language evidence has never been mentioned in Chinese laws and regulations, nor has it been admitted in Chinese courtrooms, despite some attempts made by linguistic experts (see Section 3.2.5).

China's legal system, excluding that of Hong Kong, Macau, and Taiwan, influenced by the Soviet law and characterised as a civil law system, differs from the common law system in many aspects, including laws and rules on evidence. There is no unified code of evidence law in China, and evidence-related laws are scattered across procedural laws, organic laws, and judicial interpretations. The Supreme People's Court issued a document in 2019 titled *The Nature of Persons with Expertise and Their Effectiveness in the Law of Evidence* (see He, 2021), clearly stating that there is no provision for expert witnesses in China's Civil Procedure Law and relevant judicial interpretations. Witnesses are defined as factual witnesses and do not include expert witnesses.

Unlike in the United States, where evidential rules such as the Frye and Daubert standards or Rule 702 of the Federal Rules of Evidence regulate testimony by expert witnesses, China does not have specific provisions concerning (linguistic) expert witnesses. Although in recent years the Civil Procedure Law, the Criminal Procedure Law and the New Rules of Evidence have introduced provisions on 'persons with specialized knowledge' (also called 'persons with expertise') and 'expert assistance' (also called 'expert support persons') (Wang & Liu, 2014; He, 2021; Zhang & Zhuo, 2020), the language expert or linguist as assistant to provide language evidence in court seems out of reach.

While legal scholars (Liu & Han, 2016; Liu, 2019; Song & Wan, 2021, etc.) have discussed the litigation status and effectiveness of evidence provided by 'persons with expertise' in criminal proceedings, as well as improvements to the litigation system in this regard, few studies have mentioned linguists as expert witnesses or expert supporters providing expert opinions. In judicial practice, linguists are very rarely seen testifying in court.

Due to the lack of legal regulations on language evidence, legal or forensic linguists in China have limited opportunities to participate directly in courtroom activities. As a result, Chinese legal linguistics has taken a different path from the emergence and development of forensic linguistics in common law countries like the United Kingdom and the United States.

However, it is worth noting that forensic linguistics, in its narrow sense, focusing on linguistic expert witnesses and language evidence, is emerging in China, albeit with certain limitations and challenges (see Section 3.2.5 and Sections 4.2.3 and 4.2.4).

1.3 Introducing This Element

This Element will first trace the origins of Chinese legal and forensic linguistics back to the 1980s and 1990s (Section 2), then track the progress and achievements into the 2000s (Section 3), and finally envisage the prospects of its current and future development (Section 4). One of the primary purposes of writing this Element is to inform English language readers about the Legal and Forensic Linguistics studies conducted by Chinese researchers, whose publications are mostly in Mandarin Chinese.

2 Origins in the 1980s and 1990s

The origins of Chinese legal language research in the 1980s and 1990s involved contributions from different groups of scholars. Initially, Chinese language scholars from prominent political science and law universities took the lead in this field. They became experts in legislative language consultation, fulfilling the demand for expertise in the newly established normative legal system.

During the 1990s, foreign language scholars began making significant contributions to legal language research in China. Some adopted the Western forensic linguistics research paradigm and focused on semantic and pragmatic studies of Chinese courtroom language. They explored topics such as ambiguity in courtroom language, power dynamics in judges' discourse, and courtroom questioning and response language. These scholars actively participated in international academic conferences, amplifying Chinese voices and showcasing advancements in Chinese legal language research.

Another group of foreign language scholars focused on legal translation, teaching and testing legal English, training foreign-related legal professionals, and conducting comparative analysis of Chinese and Western legal language and culture. Their research addressed the complexities of legal language in cross-cultural contexts.

Legal scholars also made notable contributions to legal language research in China. They explored the nuances of legal language usage in legal interpretation, fact-finding, conviction, and imputation. Their studies covered legal rhetoric, rule of law discourse, and the promotion of Chinese rule of law construction and culture through language.

The diversity of backgrounds and research interests among Chinese scholars, foreign language scholars, and legal scholars enriches the field of legal language studies in China. This diversity demonstrates the openness and inclusiveness of legal language research and highlights the wide-ranging applications of legal language in various societal domains.

2.1 Legal Language Studies by Chinese Language Scholars

During the 1980s and 1990s, pioneering scholars in Chinese language and law departments of political and legal institutions developed an interest in legal language due to their work demands, contributing to the field of legal linguistics in China. Noteworthy figures include Professor Pan Qingyun from East China University of Political Science and Law, Professor Wang Jie from China University of Political Science and Law, Professor Chen Jiong from Anhui University (later transferred to Jiangnan University), and Professor Jiang Jianyun from Shanghai University Law School.

While many older generation legal linguists have either passed away at a young age or are enjoying retirement, Professor Pan Qingyun and Professor Wang Jie continue to actively contribute to the field, serving as role models for current and future legal linguists. Their commitment and influence have greatly shaped the development of Legal and Forensic Linguistics in China.

2.1.1 Proposals for Establishing Legal Linguistics as a Discipline

Legal linguistics as an independent discipline was first proposed in the mid-1980s, thanks to the pioneering efforts and promotion of Cheng Jiong and Pan

Qingyun, two renowned linguists in China who played a significant role as predecessors, pioneers, and core figures in the field of legal linguistics research, making remarkable contributions and achievements for decades.

As early as 1985, **Chen Jiong** proposed the establishment of legal linguistics and published influential articles such as 'Legal linguistics should be established' (Chen, 1985a) and 'An exploration of legal linguistics' (Chen, 1985b). These articles made indelible contributions to the initiation of the discipline of legal linguistics. In his monograph *Introduction to Legal Linguistics*, published in 1998, Chen humbly wrote on the title page, 'For more than two decades, I have often worked at my desk, and my slight attainment can comfort my heart.' This heartfelt statement reflects his dedication to academic pursuits and his humble nature. Through his pioneering spirit, he inspired numerous scholars to continue building upon the foundations he established, further advancing the field of legal linguistics.

Chen (1985a: 77) defined legal linguistics as 'a discipline that combines the principles and knowledge of linguistics with the use of language in jurisprudence'. He succinctly explained the necessity and feasibility of establishing this discipline. He emphasised that Chinese law teachers increasingly recognised the need to connect language knowledge with legal practice. Chen (1985b: 49) clarified that legal linguistics is a discipline that studies legal language, combining the principles and knowledge of linguistics with the study of various legal practices and applications. It aims to explore and summarise the characteristics of legal language and address problems encountered in jurisprudence and linguistics.

Notably, in this paper, Chen mentioned the use of linguistic knowledge in case detection, somewhat similar to the research conducted by Western forensic linguists in the same period on 'author identification' and 'speaker identification'. However, it is not specified whether linguists were involved in this work, and it is presumed that investigators themselves utilised technology (such as voiceprint technology) and basic language knowledge in carrying out this work. Chen pointed out that in China, with the development of document examination techniques, linguistic knowledge (primarily dialectology) is often used in investigative cases to analyse and identify speech in criminal cases. This analysis helps determine the gender, age, origin, occupation, education, personality, and experience of the perpetrator, providing clues and directions for solving the case and serving as strong evidence for identifying the perpetrator. This may be considered the starting point of authorship analysis in forensic linguistics in China.

Chen's paper proposed a comprehensive system of legal linguistics, including comparative legal linguistics, historical legal linguistics, and descriptive legal linguistics, demonstrating forward-thinking and far-reaching perspectives. Chen (2004) provided a comprehensive review of legal language research in China over the past twenty years, dividing the early stages of legal language research in China into three periods: the gestation period, the haymaking period, and the deepening period.

Pan Qingyun has made significant contributions to legal linguistics. He completed his master's degree in theoretical linguistics under the supervision of the renowned linguist Chen Wangdao at Fudan University in 1982. Throughout his career, he focused on teaching language-related law courses, such as Legal Drafting, Legal Communication, Civil and Commercial Law, and Civil Procedure Law.

Pan's early research primarily centred around legal stylistics. Pan (1983) first proposed the concept of 'legal style' and the establishment of 'legal stylistics'. Pan (1987) further elaborated on the object, scope, and method of legal stylistics, which is akin to the register and genre studies in the systemic functional linguistics (SFL) paradigm. Notably, Pan was an early advocate for integrating 'speech spectrum analysis and speech recognition' into legal stylistics. He highlighted how these technologies could assist in determining culprits during criminal investigations (Pan, 1987: 96).

In addition to numerous articles, Pan has authored several books. In the twentieth century, he published *The Art of Legal Language* in 1989, *An Exploration of Legal Language Styles* in 1991, and *Chinese Legal Language in the Cross-Century* in 1997. Pan continued his research on legal language in the new century and published works such as *Chinese Legal Language Assessment* in 2004 and *Forensic Linguistics* in 2017. These publications showcase his ongoing dedication to studying and advancing the field of legal linguistics and will be elaborated on in Section 3.1.

It is worth noting that while Chen Jiong and Pan Qingyun proposed the establishment of legal linguistics as early as the mid-1980s, even before the concept of forensic linguistics emerged in the Western academic context, their focus was primarily on the linguistic features and rhetorical analysis of Chinese legal language. Their work was more concerned with the ontology of legislative language and broader aspects of legal language research, rather than the narrower scope of forensic linguistics as conducted by Western scholars.

2.1.2 Establishment of Legal Linguistics as a Discipline

Early proposals and calls for establishing the discipline of legal linguistics paved the way for its eventual success. In December 1998, a group of legal language researchers held an academic exchange meeting on 'the use of legal language in legal practice' in Haikou. This meeting and the subsequent academic exchange meeting on 'legal language and the construction of disciplines' held in Shanghai in June 1999 prepared the groundwork for forming an association dedicated to legal linguistics research. In July 2000, the *China Association for Forensic Linguistics* (CAFL) was formally and officially established during the 'International Symposium on Legal Language and Rhetoric' held in Shanghai. Professor Jiang Jianyun was elected as the association's first President, with Professor Liu Suzhen and Professor Wang Jie as Vice Presidents.

Jiang Jianyun, the first president of CAFL from 2000 to 2004, played a crucial role in shaping legal linguistics in China. Under his leadership, Chinese legal linguistics evolved from individual research to a collaborative community of scholars.

Despite publishing fewer works compared to Chen and Pan, Jiang's impact was equally profound. In his 1990 publication, Jiang explored the expressive nature of legal language, arguing that it encompasses not only conceptual meaning but also subjective attitudes and feelings. He analysed legal terms with emotional connotations, highlighting their evaluative nature. For example, he discussed how words like 'abet', 'seduce', and 'collude' carry emotional connotations beyond their basic meanings. Jiang recommended avoiding positive rhetorical devices in legal documents, emphasising the need for precise and unambiguous communication.

Jiang recognised the influence of context on the meaning and appropriateness of legal language. In his 1994 work, he proposed that context includes both the linguistic environment and the non-linguistic environment. He emphasised the importance of legal professionals adapting their language to suit the audience's context and needs. For instance, he suggested using plain and accessible language when communicating with illiterate defendants, aligning with the principles of the Plain Language Movement.

Jiang's contributions extended beyond legal language. He believed in studying language in conjunction with its users and the context in which it is employed. He also identified two criteria for measuring the accuracy of language use in legal activity: truthfulness and faithfulness. Truthfulness refers to aligning language use with objective reality, laws and regulations, the flow of speech, the situation, and the object of communication. Faithfulness pertains to expressing desired content of thought and achieving the desired result. These criteria provided a framework for evaluating the effectiveness and appropriateness of legal language in practice (Jiang, 1995).

Wang Jie has dedicated herself to the study of legal language for an impressive forty years. Her main work, *Legal Language Research*, published in 1999, is a comprehensive and substantial volume that covers a wide range of topics within the field of legal language. These topics include legislative language, judicial language, police interviewing and interrogation, courtroom debating and cross-examination, mediation language, and more. This extensive work has garnered high praise from renowned linguist Lu Jianming, who describes it as a unique monograph on legal language studies. Lu (2000) highlighted several key features of Wang's *Legal Language Research*. Firstly, he commended the originality of the work, noting that it showcased the author's unique analysis and insights into legal language. Wang brought a fresh perspective to the study of legal language, offering valuable contributions to the field. Secondly, the book drew on the research results of Chinese linguistics, establishing a diversified structural network for legal language research. This interdisciplinary approach laid a solid foundation for future studies in legal language. Thirdly, while Wang analysed and discussed legal language in a positive manner, she also addressed the existing problems with legal language. This balanced approach allowed for a comprehensive understanding of the subject matter. Lastly, Lu emphasised that the research results presented in this work hold direct and significant implications for legal language practice and further research in the field.

In addition to her groundbreaking research papers and monographs on legal language, Wang Jie also compiled the very first coursebook on 'forensic linguistics' in China. This coursebook, published in 1997, represents a pioneering effort in the country. 'It takes the basic theories of linguistics and jurisprudence as its framework and combines them with legislative and judicial practice by conducting scientific and standardised research on legal linguistics as an interdisciplinary subject', as introduced in Wang (1996: 90).

Qiu Daren is a pioneer in the study of legal language and has made significant contributions to the field. With a strong linguistic background from the Institute of Linguistics of the Chinese Academy of Sciences and years of experience at the Beijing Public Security Bureau, Qiu has acquired extensive knowledge and expertise in language analysis and speech identification for detecting and solving cases.

In his early work, Qiu (1980) emphasised the use of linguistic analysis to scrutinise phonetics, vocabulary, grammar, and dialects in criminal cases involving written language. This analysis helps identify important information about the perpetrators, such as their origin, age, education, and occupation. Linguistic analysis plays a crucial role in determining the direction and scope of investigations, similar to the concepts of 'authorship profiling' and 'authorship attribution' in the Western 'Forensic Authorship Analysis'.

Qiu (1981) also explored phonetic differences in Chinese dialects and their reflection in criminal cases to determine the origin and region of the perpetrators. This process is similar to speaker identification conducted by Western forensic phoneticians. Qiu's research provided numerous examples from authentic cases, illustrating the phonetic, lexical, grammatical, and dialectical features of various dialects, such as Mandarin, Hakka, Minnanese, and Cantonese.

In the early 1990s, Qiu (1991) published an article that examined the development of investigative linguistics in China. He identified three stages: the emergence period (1950s–60s), the formation period (1970s), and the development period (1980s–90s). These stages parallel the trajectory of forensic linguistics in the West. Initially, research focused on dialect issues in cases, then shifted to the recognition function of written language and its integration with criminal investigation. Finally, research focused on the identification function of language, enabling direct identification of the perpetrator through written language.

Qiu's work also highlighted the interdisciplinary nature of investigative linguistics, intersecting with sociolinguistics, dialectology, criminal investigation, and disciplines such as social psychology, neurophysiology, neuropsychology, criminal psychology, psychiatry, and judicial psychiatry.

Qiu authored two notable books: *Speech Recognition* (1985) and Investigative Linguistics (1995). *Speech Recognition* explores methods for identifying linguistic elements in case-related contexts. Qiu explained the role of language identification in case detection and covered various identification methods. *Investigative Linguistics*, the first comprehensive work in China on the theories and methods of investigative linguistics, probed the theoretical basis for identifying linguistic features and determining perpetrators. The book covered language recognition, language variation, cant, cryptic decipherment, coded language interpretation, and linguistic characteristics of mentally ill and deaf individuals.

In conclusion, Qiu Daren's contributions to legal language research and investigative linguistics have highlighted the crucial role of linguistic analysis in detecting and solving criminal cases. His meticulous examinations of linguistic elements and interdisciplinary collaboration have paved the way for further advancements in this field.

2.2 The Introduction of Forensic Linguistics into China by Foreign Language Scholars

In the late twentieth century, foreign language scholars began to play a significant role in legal language studies in China. Despite starting later than their Chinese language counterparts, these scholars made notable contributions by introducing classical works from Western forensic linguistics and conducting relevant research within the Chinese context. Following the paradigm of Western forensic linguistics, their research focused on the semantic and pragmatic aspects of Chinese courtroom language, including the examination of ambiguity, the dynamics of judges' discourse and power, and the language used in courtroom interrogations and responses. These scholars garnered attention and recognition from the legal community by applying linguistic insights to inform and enhance Chinese judicial practice. Notable figures in the foreign language community include Du Jinbang, Wu Weiping, and Liao Meizhen, who are regarded as pioneers and guiding lights in China's Legal and Forensic Linguistics fields. Their groundbreaking work provided the foundation for further advancements in studying legal language in the country.

Du Jinbang, from Guangdong University of Foreign Studies (GDUFS), is a pioneer in forensic linguistics in China. He holds the distinction of being the first master and doctoral supervisor in the field, having initiated the MA program in 1999 and enrolling PhD students in 2002. To date, he has supervised over twenty doctoral students who are actively involved in teaching legal language and conducting forensic linguistics research at various universities across the country.

Du has made significant contributions through his publications, including monographs such as Forensic Linguistics (2004), Legal Discourse Information Analysis (2014), and On Discourse Information Mining (2022), an edited tutorial on Discourse Analysis (2013), and several co-edited books on the progress and prospects of forensic linguistics in China (see Du & Yu, 2007; Du et al., 2010). He has also published over forty papers in prestigious Chinese linguistics journals, greatly enhancing our understanding of the field.

His early research focused on the disciplinary construction of forensic linguistics, as demonstrated in his seminal paper (Du, 2000) and foundational work (Du, 2004). In Du (2000), one of his most influential articles, he discussed the construction of the macro structure of forensic linguistics. Based on an overview of Western research, this article explored the research objects, theoretical principles, contents, and methods in the field. It laid the initial groundwork for the disciplinary system of forensic linguistics in China, emphasising the importance of establishing forensic linguistics as an independent discipline. By highlighting the study of language rules in various legal activities, Du has contributed to shaping the field in China. His monograph Forensic Linguistics (2004) further solidified the development of the discipline. It introduced the emergence, development, research, and practice of Western forensic linguistics and placed special emphasis on Chinese forensic linguistics and the construction of the disciplinary system within China. With its research methods, theoretical framework, and practical examples, the book has been praised for its value in establishing the disciplinary system and as a textbook for postgraduate students, as noted in Gui Shichun's preface.

Professor Du later delved into theoretical innovation, creating the DIT and its research methods and applications. These contributions represented new progress in his research, offering valuable insights into the field and will be further elaborated in Section 3.2.1. Du has also played a crucial role in establishing important resources for forensic linguistics. Under his leadership, the 'Guangwai Laboratory for Forensic Linguistics' and the 'Corpus of Legal Information Processing Systems (CLIPS)' were developed, providing platforms for research and analysis in the field. His commitment to practical research and resources is commendable.

Professor Du's contributions have been instrumental in the origin, growth, and advancement of forensic linguistics in China. His dedication to teaching, research, and the establishment of resources has had a lasting impact on the field, and his work continues to inspire and shape the future of forensic linguistics in the country.

Wu Weiping, a pioneering figure in Chinese forensic linguistics, holds the distinction of being the first scholar to introduce forensic linguistics to China and the first Chinese linguist to practice forensic linguistics, that is, to testify in US courts. He pursued his PhD in theoretical linguistics at Georgetown University in the late 1980s and early 1990s. Towards the end of his doctoral research, he enrolled in a course on language and law taught by Roger Shuy, a renowned sociolinguist and a founding father of forensic linguistics. During this time, he studied Shuy's works and approach, and became involved in the linguistic analysis of a money laundering case handled by a Philadelphia law firm. This case involved Chinese language recordings as evidence.

This case was the basis for Wu Weiping's presentation at the 1992 Law and Society annual conference. The presentation was subsequently published as an article titled 'Chinese Evidence versus the Institutional Power of English' in the journal *Forensic Linguistics* in 1995. This article was the first to analyse a Chinese corpus since the journal's inception. It examined the challenges posed by Chinese evidence (translated into English) in a courtroom where English holds a hegemonic position. The study drew upon two real-life cases (money laundering and drugs) involving secretly recorded Chinese audio tapes, in which Wu participated as a consultant and expert witness. The study revealed that the unique linguistic features of Chinese are often overlooked during translation, leading to doubts about the credibility of evidence in court. For instance, the article focused on the polysemy of the word 'gei' in the money laundering case. Specifically, it examined the Cantonese phrase 'give money to somebody', which consists of a verb and a preposition, and how its translation into English as 'give money, gave somebody' strengthens the impropriety of the defendant's actions. The incorrect translation failed to convey the intended meaning that the money was given to a specific person. The article also analysed the tense of 'give' in its English translation, highlighting how the prosecution's linguistic evidence mistranslated instances of 'give' as past tense. This misinterpretation further misled the jury and resulted in an incorrect verdict.

Additionally, sociocultural factors associated with Chinese are frequently disregarded in legal contexts where language plays a pivotal role. For example, in analysing the use of 'four-letter words' such as (f**k) by the defendant towards his accomplice in the drug case, the prosecuting attorney questioned the prevalence of such cursing in a conversation between two friends. Wu explained that the English translation of the linguistic evidence failed to capture the sociocultural elements embedded in the original text and the subcultural context of the criminal gang. Within criminal gangs, the use of vulgar language is a subcultural norm that signifies closeness among gang members, rather than literal cursing as perceived by lawyers. In many cultures, the formality of language is influenced by the level of closeness in interpersonal relationships. Close individuals communicate more casually and may even use vulgar language, particularly among less-educated gang members. In conclusion, the study highlighted the lack of attention paid by judges, juries, and lawyers to the specific challenges posed by Chinese evidence in court.

This article catapulted Wu Weiping to prominence and stands as a masterpiece of linguistic evidence analysis. Since then, he has been involved in linguistic consultation and analysis for various cases, including smuggling and commercial theft cases, further advancing forensic linguistics in its narrow sense. He has also published several papers in domestic journals referencing Western forensic linguistics, conferences, institutions, and journals. Notable works include an introduction to research methods in forensic linguistics (2002a), a proposal for a disciplinary classification of forensic linguistics encompassing oral, written, and bilingual studies (2002b), and the publication of the monograph 'Language and the Law: Linguistic Research in the Legal Field' (2002c). These contributions have enhanced our understanding of legal language and made significant contributions to the development of forensic linguistics in China.

Liao Meizhen is a distinguished figure in Chinese forensic linguistics, known for his pioneering work in the empirical study of courtroom discourse. In the late 1990s, Liao decided to pursue his doctoral degree under the guidance of Professor Gu Yueguo at the Chinese Academy of Social Sciences. He dedicated himself to forensic linguistics, with a particular focus on courtroom discourse. During his doctoral studies, he visited various courts to observe trials, collecting a substantial amount of first-hand data.

Professor Liao completed his theoretical doctoral dissertation, which was published as a monograph titled *A Study on Courtroom Questions, Responses, and their Interaction: A Linguistic Perspective* (Liao, 2003). This book is devoted to studying and analysing question-response interaction at both micro and macro levels in trials in the Chinese courtroom. Mr Lu Jianming, a famous linguist who wrote the preface to the book, pointed out that 'the study of courtroom question-response is of great practical significance and theoretical value to the improvement of the quality of judges and lawyers, as well as to the study of the Chinese language ontology' and praised that the book 'fills the blank in this area'. Transcripts of tape recordings of thirteen courtroom trials amounting to more than 900,000 words were used as data, of which questions and responses were identified and then studied and analysed within a framework which draws insights from speech act theory, discourse analysis, conversation analysis and corpus linguistics. This book was innovative in that the author put forward a theoretical model called 'the principle of goal and goal analysis in human action' to complement Grice's classical Cooperative Principle. Thus, 'cooperation or non-co-operation is a choice made by the participants in a conversational activity, and this choice is governed first and foremost by goals'. The Principle of Goal is a prerequisite for using the principle of cooperation. This book points out that the participants' goals are the dividing line and the criterion for the suitability of the principle of cooperation, and that it is only when the goals are the same that the participants follow the principle of cooperation. The Principle of Goal has a strong explanatory power because it can be further sublimated into a criterion for judging the coherence of the discourse: if the response is directed to the goal of the question, it is coherent, and as long as the response does not address the goal of the question, it is not coherent. Professor Liao's theoretical innovation of the Principle of Goal will be expanded on in Section 3.2.2.

Additionally, Professor Liao utilised the surplus data in the corpus to write a practical book titled 'Trial Communication Strategies', which has seen three editions (Liao, 2004, 2005, 2009). This book extended the findings of forensic linguistics to legal practitioners, providing guidance for their judicial practice, and covering topics such as questioning, responding, and presupposing strategies employed by judges, prosecutors, and lawyers respectively. Unlike a fragmented guide to practical techniques, this applied research offered a more constructive approach. The successive reprints of the book serve as a testament to the broad prospects of applying theoretical insights from forensic linguistics to judicial practice.

3 Progress in the 2000s

This section will examine the progress in Legal and Forensic Linguistics in the 2000s. It begins by introducing continuous contributions by the early pioneers in the field of language and law studies, then delves into the new development of forensic linguistics by foreign language researchers. Topics include the DIT, the Principle of Goal, Functional Forensic Discourse Analysis, Legal Discourse as a Social Process, empirical studies on language evidence, and legal translation and interpreting studies.

3.1 Progress in Language and Law Studies

As we progress through this new century, the dedication and unwavering commitment of early pioneers in the Chinese language community must be commended. Pan Qingyun and Wang Jie, among others, stand out as prominent models who have left an indelible mark in the field of language and law studies. Their relentless pursuit of knowledge and prolific writing demonstrated their passion and expertise. These remarkable individuals deserve recognition for their valuable contributions.

3.1.1 Contributions by Professor Pan Qingyun

Pan's book, *Chinese Legal Language Assessment*, published in December 2004 by the Chinese Dictionary Publishing House, offers a comprehensive and scientific evaluation of the Chinese legal language. It explores the nature, characteristics, and research methods of legal language, as well as its application in legislation, legal documents, criminal investigation, courtroom debates, and more. The book draws on knowledge from various disciplines and combines it with the practice of legislation, judiciary, and the construction of a democratic legal system in China.

The book is divided into three parts. The first part, 'Review of Legal Language Cognition', examined the origin and development of legal language as an independent discipline in China and other countries. The second part, 'Contemporary Chinese Legal Language Assessment', provided a thorough study of the characteristics, structure, and operational mechanisms of contemporary Chinese legal language. It also explored its application techniques in various legal contexts. The third part, 'Development of Chinese Legal Language', examined the relationship between legal language and judicial justice, legal system reform, bilingual legal language in Hong Kong and Macau, and legal language in Taiwan.

Chinese Legal Language Assessment is a remarkable book that offers valuable insights into legal language. The author's extensive research and interdisciplinary approach make it a valuable resource. The book's structure allows for a comprehensive understanding of legal language and its application in different legal domains. The arguments presented are well-documented, rigorous, and innovative. Furthermore, the author's fluent writing style enhances the book's readability. Overall, it is an indispensable resource for anyone studying legal language in China.

In addition to this monumental work, Pan has written several short articles to popularise the research on Chinese and English legal language. Despite specialising in theoretical linguistics with a Chinese language background, Pan possesses proficient English skills and excels in engaging with foreign forensic linguistic researchers. During a personal visit to John Gibbons, they discussed legal language studies in China, forensic linguistics in the West, and Pan's particular interest in the language disadvantages individuals face within legal systems. This visit inspired Pan to write two articles in 2019 on these topics.

Pan's article titled 'A Comparative Examination of the Past and Present Chinese and English Legal Languages and Their Reform and Optimization' (Pan, 2019a) was a comparative study to identify the characteristics and limitations of Chinese and English legal languages. He proposed methods for reforming and optimising these languages, aiming to promote mutual understanding, leverage strengths, standardise weaknesses, and enhance judicial cooperation and legal–cultural exchanges. Pan highlighted issues such as the frequent use of remote meanings, archaic words, jargon, ceremonial terms, and cryptic expressions in legal English, which result in obscurity and redundancy. To address this, Pan suggested adopting the 'Plain English Movement' advocated by Mellinkoff (1963), which emphasises accuracy, conciseness, clarity, and durability in legal language. Regarding China's legal language problem, Pan attributed it to legislative and judicial language 'anomie' and the arbitrary and conflicting nature of legal language. His proposed solutions included standardising legal language, eliminating outdated and ambiguous terms, ensuring strict correspondence between legal terms and concepts, incorporating and standardising useful legal terms from major legal systems worldwide, and abandoning politically and morally charged preaching, slang, and terminology from the Cultural Revolution era.

In another article titled 'The Language Dilemma of the "Valley People" Facing the Law' (Pan, 2019b), Pan explored the difficulties and language barriers faced by disadvantaged individuals (the poor and weak) when encountering the law. Using Li Yu's term 'valley people' to refer to those with low social and economic status, Pan presented specific cases to illustrate this group's linguistic challenges in dealing with legal issues. The insights from this short article were further elaborated in his article titled 'The Legal Embarrassment and Language Problems Faced by Vulnerable Groups' (Pan, 2019c). Pan pointed out that language serves as a 'double-edged sword', acting as both a vehicle and a 'prison' for justice. For disadvantaged groups, law-related language creates insurmountable gaps. The article discussed ways to implement discourse rights for these groups, alleviate their language barriers, and address their legal difficulties to achieve judicial justice. Pan emphasised the need to protect the discourse rights of this group, improve their legal difficulties, and proposed specific measures such as strengthening the legal supervision of the judiciary and incorporating the full enjoyment of litigation rights, language rights, and discourse rights into the supervisory vision. This concern for the language capacity of vulnerable groups was also evident in Pan's conference paper titled 'Language Rights Comprehensive Protection of Juvenile Criminal Defendants in the Context of Rule-by-Law' presented at the 12th Biennial Conference of the International Association for Forensic Linguists (IAFL12) held in Guangzhou, China in 2015 (see www.flrchina.com/001/108.htm).

3.1.2 Contributions by Professor Wang Jie

Despite her advanced age, Professor Wang Jie's passion for the language of law remains undiminished, and she continues to write. In one of her works from 2004, she explored the interactive language used in accusatorial courtroom trials, pointing out that 'although China's criminal courts have transitioned from an inquisitorial to an accusatorial trial context, the trial language still carries remnants of the inquisitorial trial and struggles to balance the pursuit of truth and the exercise of power' (Wang, 2004: 77). In Wang (2010), she reflected on the progress of legal language research in mainland China over the past thirty years, focusing on legislative language, judicial language, legal language teaching, and the training of new legal talent. She noted that legal language research in China has evolved alongside the development of Chinese society, shifting from a focus on the 'legal system' to the 'rule of law', driven by societal needs. Wang Jie stressed the fusion of law and language, content and form in legal language research. She suggested conducting both static research on the discourse system of legal language and dynamic variation research on the application of legal language. Modern and scientific methods, such as statistical quantification and ranking clustering, can be employed to study the discourse system of legal language using legal language corpora. Detailed analysis and description from grammatical, semantic, and pragmatic perspectives can be conducted on specific legal language corpora. Wang Jie also provided a comprehensive overview of early works in forensic linguistics in China before 2000, as well as new influential works that emerged in the first decade of the twenty-first century.

Law-Language-Linguistic Diversity, edited by Wang Jie in 2006, is a collection of academic papers presented at the 9th International Symposium on Law and Language. The symposium centred around the legal protection of diverse languages, the linguistic freedom of individuals, linguistic equality among nations, and how languages can serve legislation and justice. The proceedings of the conference encompassed twelve topics, including the relationship between language rights, language equality, and linguistic diversity in the context of protecting language rights and achieving language equality. It also dealt with the protection of minority languages, various types of language legislation, legal documents on international language rights, language diversity, language legislation and policy in diverse contexts, and language and law issues in multilingual societies. Other areas included the influence of social and cultural factors on linguistic diversity and resulting legal challenges, the study of legal language and the discipline of forensic linguistics, linguistic standardisation of legal texts, linguistic issues in the translation of legal texts, and finally the challenges of language and writing in legal activities.

Wang Jie's recent interaction with Zhang Jun, the former Procurator General of the Supreme Procuratorate and the incumbent Chief Justice of the People's Supreme Court of China, is noteworthy. Inspired by an interview transcript of Zhang published in the *Legal Daily* on 12 May 2020, Wang wrote an article titled 'The Legality and Humanity in the Interview of the Procurator General of the Supreme Procuratorate'. In this article, Wang analysed Zhang's language use and its impact on laypeople, highlighting his successful integration of legal reasoning, emotional language, and rational judicial language. Procurator General Zhang Jun appreciated Wang's linguistic analysis and was interviewed by her, resulting in the publication of 'The Best Legal Language is the Social Language and Living Language Spoken by Legal People – Excerpts from Professor Wang Jie's Interview with Procurator General Zhang Jun' in the *Rule of Law News Communication.*

During the interview, Zhang Jun made several key points. Firstly, he emphasised that effectively using legal language requires sentiment and respect for the parties involved. Understanding and connecting with people emotionally is important in legal communication. Secondly, he highlighted the significance of language ability, stating that understanding what people say and choosing the right words are essential for effective legal language use. Thirdly, Zhang Jun emphasised that confidence in using legal language comes from understanding the person you are communicating with and their language environment, and then adapting your language accordingly. By combining sentiment, ability, and confidence, legal professionals can create a significant impact through their language. Lastly, Zhang Jun claimed that the best legal language is the language of society and life spoken by legal professionals. He encouraged legal professionals to transform legal language, regulations, and thinking into accessible language that resonates with people's everyday lives.

Professor Wang Jie deserves applause for her insightful analysis and dedication to the study of legal language. Her linguistic analysis of Zhang Jun's interview showcased the importance of effectively using language in the legal domain and the significance of language in the legal profession. Their interaction serves as an inspiration to further explore the intersection of law and language, promoting a better understanding of legal concepts and fostering effective communication between legal professionals and the general public.

As we continue navigating an increasingly diverse and interconnected world, studying law and language remains essential. It is through the dedicated efforts of scholars like Pan Qinyun and Wang Jie that we can better appreciate the nuances and complexities of legal language, ensuring that justice is accessible, comprehensible, and fair to all.

3.2 Development of Forensic Linguistics in China

Entering the new century, forensic linguistics has experienced rapid growth due to the tireless research efforts of foreign language scholars in China. Notably, Du Jingbang, Liao Meizhen, Wang Zhenhua, Yuan Chuanyou, and others have made significant strides in disciplinary construction, theoretical innovation, and practical applications of theories in the field.

3.2.1 Contributions by Professor Du Jinbang and Discourse Information Theory (DIT)

Du Jingbang's contributions to the disciplinary construction and mentorship of young scholars in forensic linguistics at the GDUFS led to his election as the second President of the Chinese Association for Forensic Linguistics (CAFL) in 2004. As a result, GDUFS became the permanent venue for the association's secretariat.

In addition to his own research, Du Jingbang dedicated a considerable amount of time and effort to mentoring young scholars who pursued doctoral research in various areas of forensic linguistics under his supervision. Notable monographs based on their doctoral theses have been published, including Yuan's (2010) study on police interrogation, Zhang's (2011) exploration of lawyer evaluation, Zhao's (2011) investigation of information structure and language realisation in legal discourse, Chen's (2011) analysis of judges' trial discourse processing, Ge's (2013) examination of courtroom questioning, Ge's (2018) study on Civil Court hearings, and Xu's (2013) research on court conciliation, just to mention a few.

Under Professor Du's guidance, several PhD graduates have received research project funding from the National Social Science Foundation of China. These projects include topics such as the multimodal study of new media discourse on legal literacy, social cognition of courtroom discourse, research on online judicial opinion discourse based on evaluation theory, research on translation legislation from the perspective of national strategy, research of corpus-based discourse identification of telecommunication fraud, research on social media users' language fingerprint identification and language fingerprint database construction, and research on the corpus-based rule of law communication discourse of the Communist Party of China in the past century. These monographs and projects have significantly advanced the development of forensic linguistics in China, and Professor Du Jingbang's contributions have been invaluable.

Apart from these achievements, Professor Du has devoted himself to developing a new theory called Discourse Information Theory since 2005. Forensic linguistics, which combines the fields of law and language, plays a crucial role in promoting justice by identifying, analysing, and resolving language-related issues in legal activities (Du, 2004: 18). Over the past three decades, forensic linguistics has benefited from various theories, particularly those from the field of linguistics. Equipped with a 'linguistic toolkit' (Coulthard et al., 2017: 121), forensic linguists have provided language evidence to the court and offered valuable insights to legal professionals. However, to fully realise its potential as an independent discipline and make significant contributions to society in the twenty-first century, there is an urgent need for a theory specifically tailored to forensic linguistics (Xu, 2016).

Among the efforts made in this regard, Professor Du Jinbang has proposed the DIT (Du, 2007, 2011, 2014, 2022). This theory offers a fresh perspective on analysing legal discourse and provides a theoretical framework for examining information structures, contents, and relationships at a broader discourse level. The DIT has found wide acceptance and application across various branches of forensic linguistics (Du, 2022: 24). This section will explain the fundamentals of the DIT and explore its applications in forensic linguistics.

(1) The basics of the DIT

The DIT draws on various sources, including studies on linguistic information (Mathesius,1929; Prince,1981), discourse structures (van Dijk & Kintsch, 1983; Roberts, 1996; Büring, 1999), communication models (Lasswell, 1948; Braddock, 1958), and knowledge categories (Labov & Fanshel, 1977; van Dijk, 2008). This theory paves a new way for the study of forensic linguistics by offering fresh insights and approaches. In the following discussion, working definitions of discourse and information in the DIT will be presented first, followed by a brief introduction to the macro tree information structure, where detailed information properties will be introduced.

Discourse: The DIT views discourse as an umbrella term encompassing written and spoken texts. It considers discourse as a continuum, regardless of its size or medium. By exploring the common features of different types of legal discourse across languages, the DIT ensures the compatibility of the theory in forensic linguistics. Additionally, the DIT recognises the social nature of discourse, acknowledging it as both a product of social activities and a tool for influencing society.

Information: In contrast to the systemic functional view that analyses information at the clause level (Hu, 1994), the DIT takes a discourse perspective. It defines information as propositions, which are minimal communication units with relatively independent and complete structures. This definition highlights the semantic, pragmatic, and cognitive attributes of information, enabling the DIT-based analysis to not only depict the linguistic features of legal texts, but also provide cognitive and psychological explanations of language use within them.

Macro information tree structure: According to the DIT, each discourse can be seen as a hierarchical network resembling an information tree. At the top of this tree is the kernel proposition, serving as the trunk carrying the main idea of the discourse. Detailed information units at lower levels further develop this idea. Each information unit corresponds to a proposition, which can be an incomplete sentence or a question. These information units act as carriers of different properties of discourse information. Furthermore, each information unit can be further divided into three types of information elements: process, entity, and condition.

Figure 1 illustrates the structure of the information tree in the DIT. It visually represents how the discourse unfolds, with the kernel proposition at the centre. This structure facilitates the exchange of information within the discourse, ensuring coherence. The DIT's framework systematically analyses legal texts, considering the levels, combinations, and the linguistic realisation of information elements. It also allows for exploring how discourse users achieve their communicative purpose of influencing cognition, attitude, or behaviour at a cognitive level.

In the DIT, the relationship between an information unit and its higher-level unit is referred to as an 'information knot'. Like branches in a tree, these knots connect the information units (leaves) to the trunk, ensuring coherence throughout the discourse. There are fifteen types of information knots, which are

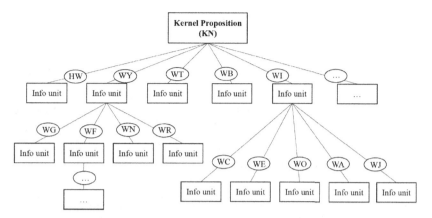

Figure 1 The information tree structure (Du, 2007).

represented by various interrogative abbreviations: WT (what thing), WB (what basis), WF (what fact), WI (what inference), WP (what disposal), WO (who), WN (when), WR (where), HW (how), WY (why), WE (what effect), WC (what cause), WA (what attitude), WG (what change), and WJ (what judgement).

In the same way that trees transport water and nutrients, the discourse information tree also exhibits different patterns of information flow. The communicative needs, roles, and competence of discourse users influence the information flow within a discourse. Analysing the categories of information sharing (whether information is known to only one person or both) and the types of information flow helps uncover the discourse dynamics.

To summarise, the information tree structure in the DIT vividly represents the macrostructure of discourse. Each genre of legal texts exhibits unique tree structures, and analysing these structures can reveal similarities and differences between the legal texts. Additionally, studying the types and functions of information knots, levels and combinations of information units, and the linguistic realisation of information elements contributes to a systematic description of legal texts. Furthermore, by focusing on information as the stable intersection, linguistic features of legal texts can be analysed at the surface-level, uncovering how discourse users achieve their communicative purpose of changing cognition, attitude, or behaviour at the cognitive level.

(2) Applications of the DIT

Aiming to provide a theoretical framework for forensic linguistics, the DIT highly values its potential to guide theoretical construction and to be applied in different settings of legal language. To date, the DIT has been utilised as the main theoretical basis in twelve doctoral dissertations at the GDUFS, leading to the development of DIT-based models. Some of these models have been published in the *International Journal of Speech, Language, and the Law*. For example, the DIT-based Frame Model (Chen, 2011) focuses on how judges can reconstruct a rational prosecution–defence–judge relationship through effective discourse information processing. The DIT-based Persuasion Model (Xu, 2014) explores how persuasion is realised in court conciliation through information exchange. The DIT-based Analytical Framework (Zhang, 2016) studies the authorship attribution of Chinese legal texts. In addition, some of these doctoral dissertations have also been published by international publishing houses. For instance, the DIT-based Cognitive Model (Ge, 2018) investigates how judges employ discourse information to help parties resolve conflicts, while the DIT-based Multimodal Teaching Model (Huai, 2021) analyses how teachers utilise multimodal discourse information in teaching.

In addition to the DIT-based models, the DIT has also been widely applied to the analysis of legislative discourse, courtroom discourse, police interrogation, legal translation and interpreting, authorship analysis, forensic speaker identification, legal language teaching, witness credibility analysis, and public legal education discourse (Yuan, Xu & Zhang, 2024).

a. Macroanalysis of the information tree structure

When conducting a DIT-based study, analysing the macro information tree structure is a typical starting point. This analysis aims to describe the discourse features of a specific genre of legal discourse, compare features across different legal genres, and evaluate the quality of academic writing (Du, 2007, 2009).

One aspect of this analysis involves comparing the number of information levels and units in different genres. For example, a comparison between courtroom discourse and legislative discourse reveals that while courtroom discourse may have fewer first-level information units, it tends to have more information levels and a higher density of information (Du, 2007). The density and sequence of information can also be examined to identify any potential omissions of important information (Du, 2014).

Additionally, the frequencies of information knots and how information units are combined provide insights into legal activities. For instance, in a study on court conciliation, Xu (2014) identifies three types of discourse information: factual (WF/WT), attitudinal (WA/HW), and procedural (WP/WB/WJ). She observes that these three types of information often co-occur in court conciliation, ensuring that persuasion is grounded in facts, respect for parties' free will, and adherence to legal procedures. Therefore, the absence of a particular type of discourse information may raise questions about the effectiveness of persuasive efforts. The example cited from Xu (2013: 83) illustrates how factual information paves the way for ensuing persuasive efforts.

1. **Judge:** $<WF^1>$ Both the plaintiff and the defendants used to live together for about 10 years.
2. $<WF^2>$ There should have been certain affection between them.
3. $<WF^3>$ The plaintiff has performed partial duties to raise the defendants.
4. $<WF^4>$ Now, the plaintiff leads a difficult life.
5. $<WA^1>$ The defendants should provide the plaintiff with some help.
6. $<WA^2>$ Meanwhile, the plaintiff has to consider the actual situations and economic capacities of the two defendants.
7. $<WA^3>$ Can both parties negotiate the amount of maintenance?
8. **Plaintiff:** $<WA^3>$ Yes, I agree.
9. **Defendants:** $<WA^3>$ We can provide a certain amount of money.

This extract is taken from a dispute over maintenance where the plaintiff, a stepfather, demands support from the defendants, his two stepchildren. During the trial, it was found that the plaintiff raised the defendants for about ten years when they were underage. He is now over sixty years old and experiences economic difficulties in daily life. After a court investigation and debate, the trial judge inquires whether both parties are willing to proceed with mediation. However, instead of directly asking for their willingness to mediate in line 7, the judge uses four factual information units (WF in lines 1–4) and two attitudinal information units (WA in lines 5 and 6). The combination of factual and attitudinal information units lays a solid ground for further persuasive efforts.

Factual information enables parties to get a better understanding of the case. It describes what has happened in the case and guides parties to reflect upon the past events and look for a better solution to their disputes. As can be seen from the example, the three factual information units (WF1, WF3, and WF4) introduce the facts that have been presented during the trial. These facts echo requirements set forth in Article 1067 of the Civil Code of the People's Republic of China, which prescribes that 'If children who have come of age fail to perform their duty, or if parents are unable to work or have difficulty in providing for themselves, they shall have the right to demand support payments from their children.' The aforementioned three factual information paves the way for the coming attitude (WA1) of the court that the defendants should support the plaintiff (line 5).

In addition to the factual information units which resort to logical appeal, the inferred fact (WF2 in line 2) relies on emotional appeal. It provides a common ground for both parties to mediate and 'generates an air of optimism, mutuality and confidence' (Boulle, 2005: 197). The inferred fact (line 2) emphasises affection between both parties, setting a common ground for the judge's coming subjective attitude (WA2) that the plaintiff has to consider the reality and economic capabilities of the defendants. Judging by both parties' replies to the judge's inquiry in lines 8 and 9, it can be found that a combination of factual and attitudinal information enhances mutual understanding and is conducive to the ensuing mediation.

DIT-based studies uncover valuable information about discourse features, information distribution, and combinations in different legal contexts through the macroanalysis of the information tree structure. This analysis helps researchers gain a deeper understanding of the dynamics and effectiveness of legal communication.

b. Micro information elements analysis

In addition to the macroanalysis of the information tree structure, the DIT also employs microanalysis of information elements to uncover various aspects of legal discourse. This microanalysis helps understand how legal translators and interpreters reorganise information (Tian, 2008), how prosecutors present illegal activities carried out by defendants (Pan & Du, 2011), how points of adjudication in guiding cases are summarised (Huang, 2021), and how judges summarise issues based on different accounts from parties in court (Guo, 2022).

The DIT analyses discourse information based on propositions and incorporates the perspective of case grammar to classify information elements in detail. Case grammar suggests that people or things can have multiple roles in a specific process, and these roles remain relatively stable despite surface-level differences in language expression (Fillmore, 1968). Based on the roles played by information elements in the process, the DIT classifies five types of entities: Agent, Dative, Patient, Factitive, and Beneficent (Du, 2014: 89). The Agent is the doer of the process, while the Dative is the animate being affected by the process.

For example, consider the dialogue between a prosecutor and a defendant in a case involving illegal medical practice (Pan & Du, 2011):

> Prosecutor: After you have been penalised by the administrative department, why did **you** keep practising medicine?

Defendant: **Fellow villagers** came to me.

Prosecutor: Whom did **you** treat?

Defendant: **Fellow villager XX** asked me for a medical treatment.

In this extract, the analysis focuses on the entities, specifically the Agent and Dative. The comparison of the roles played by the prosecutor ('you') and the defendant reveals a power dynamic and resistance during the questioning. While the prosecutor takes the defendant as the subject of the sentence, emphasising the defendant's active role, the defendant shifts the attention to the 'fellow villagers' and presents himself as the object of their actions.

Through this microanalysis of information elements, the DIT uncovers subtle nuances and power dynamics within legal discourse, providing insights into the strategies different participants employ in the legal process.

c. Future directions of the DIT

The DIT has shown great vitality through the publication of monographs such as *Legal Discourse Information* (Du, 2014), *Methodology of Forensic Linguistics* (Du & Ge, 2016), and *Information Mining of Legal Discourse* (Du, 2022), as well as numerous doctoral theses and papers. As information technology and artificial intelligence continue to advance, China has been actively promoting the development of smart justice, including automatic contract generation, automatic judgement generation, and automatic court transcript generation. One of the major challenges in smart justice is how to effectively process information and generate normative discourse.

The DIT is still evolving and flourishing as a theory tailored to forensic linguistics. Further research may focus on expanding the current corpus, known as the Corpus of Legal Information Processing, as well as developing methods for automatic tagging of discourse information and conducting interdisciplinary analysis of discourse information. It is hoped that the DIT can contribute more to smart justice and improve the delivery of justice in legal systems.

The future of the DIT looks promising, and its continued development and application have the potential to boost the field of forensic linguistics and enhance the efficiency and fairness of legal processes.

3.2.2 Contributions by Professor Liao Meizhen and Principle of Goal

After completing his PhD dissertation and publishing his monographs in the early 2000s, Professor Liao Meizhen began to actively participate in the international academic community. As a Fulbright Research Scholar, he was invited to deliver academic lectures at prestigious institutions such as Brooklyn Law

School, Loyola Law School in Los Angeles, University of California, Santa Barbara, and University of California, San Diego in 2006 and 2007. Liao also attended the 6th Biennial Conference of the IAFL held at the University of Sydney, Australia in 2003, the 8th Biennial Conference held at Seattle University, Washington, USA in 2007, and delivered a keynote speech at the 12th Biennial Conference held at GDUFS, Guangzhou, China in 2015.

Liao has produced abundant research results and has published over sixty academic papers in addition to his monographs. Notable works in English include Liao (2009c) on interruptions in Chinese criminal courtroom discourse, Liao (2012b) on courtroom discourse in China, Liao (2013b) on the power dynamics of interruption, and Liao (2015) on speech and silence within and beyond language and law. The article 'A study of interruptions in Chinese criminal court discourse' published in *Text & Talk* is particularly noteworthy. This article examined interruptions in Chinese criminal court discourse using court transcripts from four Chinese criminal courts as a corpus. The study focused on the frequency, function, causes, and distribution of interruptions, and their relationship to the Chinese legal system and legal culture. The findings highlighted a substantial asymmetry in the interruptions in Chinese court trials, with prosecutors interrupting the most, defence lawyers interrupting the least, and judges falling in between. The author explained this imbalance in terms of China's judicial system and legal culture and compared interruptions in Chinese criminal trials with those in American courtrooms.

Liao's productivity is even more remarkable in his Chinese writings, with over fifty papers mainly related to legal language, courtroom discourse, interruption, and the Principle of Goal. Some of his early representative articles include Liao (2002) on the status quo of Chinese courtroom trials from a linguistic perspective, Liao (2004b) on the Principle of Goal and cooperation in interactive courtroom discourse, Liao (2006) on 'Formulation' in Chinese courtroom interaction, and Liao (2007) on the application of the principle of cooperation in legislative communication.

These articles report on an in-depth study of 'interactive courtroom discourse', particularly the phenomenon of interruptions (Liao, 2004b, 2009c, 2013b). The main points highlighted include:

(1) Courtroom interruptions serve four main functions: control, dominance, competition, and cooperation. Interruptions in the courtroom primarily aim to exert control and dominance, resulting in conflict and confrontation as the main outcomes, while cooperation plays a secondary role.

(2) Judges and prosecutors have the highest proportion of interrupting others' speech among courtroom participants, and the overall characteristic of

these interruptions is conflict. Judges' interruptions can be procedural or substantive, involving both intervention as a third-party arbitrator and implementation as an entity investigator. However, the proportion of the latter is higher than the former.

(3) In civil trials, interruptions are primarily attributed to judges, while in criminal trials, judges and prosecutors are the main interrupters. Interruptions also serve as a strategy. Interruptions between defense counsel and defendants are rare and predominantly cooperative. Interruptions in cross-examinations are predominantly adversarial, while interruptions in direct questioning are minimal and mostly cooperative.

(4) The reasons for interruptions are as follows: excessive speech, prompting, irrelevant speech, verification or clarification of information, and verbose or redundant speech.

(5) The study of interruption phenomena in courtroom discourse involves not only linguistic issues but also procedural and substantive justice issues, rights, power, and the rule of law.

(6) There is a close relationship between courtroom interruptions and impoliteness. The degree of impoliteness varies systematically based on interruption patterns, interruption location, accompanying speech behaviour, the function of interruption, and the roles of courtroom participants. The formation of impoliteness is influenced by legal systems, courtroom roles, legal culture, and other factors.

Furthermore, the author also conducted research on the interruption phenomenon in criminal courtrooms and gender, finding that 'women exhibit more aggression and power than men in the courtroom. Moreover, women with higher status and positions of greater power demonstrate a more assertive demeanour in professional activities compared to men' (Liao, 2015: 54). The author further analysed the reasons behind this, pointing out that

> due to the adversarial trial model we practice and the traditional presumption of guilt, legal professionals tend to perceive defendants as 'criminals' or 'wrongdoers'. Additionally, due to the historically disadvantaged position of women, they seem to feel the need to display assertiveness in order to effectively dominate and control such a highly instrumental activity as courtroom adjudication. With the deepening reform of judicial trial methods and the increasing emphasis on procedural justice, this situation should undergo changes (Liao, 2015: 54).

In disciplinary construction, Liao's (2004a) article titled 'A Review of the Study of Forensic Linguistics Abroad', published in *Contemporary Linguistics*, was particularly instructive. This paper is a review of forensic linguistics abroad with an emphasis on the period after the 1970s and on countries where the Anglo-American law system is practised, specifically the United States and Australia. The examination was organised around three perspectives, namely the study of language as an object, process, and instrument, which also characterised the process of forensic linguistics abroad or represented the three stages in the development of the discipline. This high-quality review article offers a comprehensive and systematic overview of the prominent figures, research fields, and achievements in forensic linguistics abroad.

The article begins by highlighting the significance of Mellinkoff's (1963) masterpiece, *Legal Language*, as the classic work on the ontology of legal language. It points out that Mellinkoff's book was the first comprehensive and in-depth study of English and American legal languages, making it an influential work in the history of legal language studies. Furthermore, the book was crucial in promoting the 'plain English movement' in law during the 1970s.

The article then examines the research trends and priorities in legal language studies after the 1970s. During this period, the focus shifted to courtroom discourse and oral interaction in legal activities. The research interests revolved around three main areas: legal language as a process, legal language as an instrument, and the involvement of linguists in providing linguistic evidence in legal interactions. The author provides a detailed overview of the main researchers' contributions during this period. For example, Charrow and Charrow's (1979) study on 'jury instructions', Levi and Walker's (1990) and O'Barr's (1982) research on courtroom discourse strategies, discourse styles, and structures, as well as studies on legal language as a process by Atkinson and Drew (1979), Bennett and Feldman (1981), and Stygall (1994). Studies on legal language as an instrument include Matoesian's (1993) and Conley and O'Barr's (1998) works on power dynamics in rape and divorce trials, Walsh's (1994) and Eades' (1994) works on Aboriginal land rights litigation, and Luchjenbroers' (1997) study on the power dynamics of witnesses (defendants). The article also highlights studies on applying linguistic evidence in legal trials, including Jones' (1994) research on legal phonology and Eagleson's (1994) investigation of written spelling, diction, grammatical morphology, and syntactic structure. At the discourse level, the article discusses Shuy's (1987) analysis of recorded evidence, Berk-Seligson's (1990) study on legal translation, and Hibbitts' (1994) examination of visual and auditory metaphors in American law and legal practice.

Overall, the article offers a comprehensive and objective overview of the key figures, major research areas, and practical applications in legal linguistics over the past century. It serves as a valuable reference for domestic legal linguistics researchers and enthusiasts, particularly for Chinese forensic linguistics scholars. However, one limitation of the article was its overemphasis on

American and Australian scholars, neglecting the contributions of British forensic linguists like Coulthard, who is considered the founder of the discipline and has made significant contributions.

Another significant contribution by Professor Liao Meizhen is his role as the Forensic Linguistics Translation Series Editor. This series aims to translate classical works on foreign forensic linguistics into Chinese and publish them through Law Press. The seven translations include Conley and Obar's *Law, Language, and Power* (2007), Solan's *The Language of Judges* (2007), Goodrich's *Legal Discourse* (2007), Bix's *Law, Language, and Legal Certainty* (2007), Gibbons' *Introduction to Forensic Linguistics* (2007), Melinkoff's *The Language of Law* (2014), and Tiersma's *Legal Language* (2014). The publication of these translations has undeniably expanded the horizons of the Chinese forensic linguistics community and advanced the research and development of the discipline. It provides an excellent opportunity for legal linguists in the Chinese-speaking community, who may not have direct access to the original texts, to understand the field of foreign forensic linguistics. Moreover, it promotes the exchange and mutual learning between Chinese and foreign legal linguists and legal linguists in the Chinese-speaking and foreign language communities in China.

Professor Liao's editorship of the Forensic Linguistics Translation Series has significantly impacted the accessibility and development of forensic linguistics in China. By translating and publishing these seven classical works, Professor Liao has provided Chinese legal linguists with a valuable resource to enhance their understanding of foreign forensic linguistics. This not only facilitated their research and academic growth but also promoted cross-cultural exchanges and mutual learning between Chinese and international legal linguists.

Throughout Liao's study of courtroom discourse, he placed great importance on theoretical innovation and enhancement. Particularly, he proposed the 'principle of goal direction and discourse analysis', later developed into the 'Principle of Goal' or simply 'Goal Principle'. This principle asserted that any rational and normal speech behaviour of individuals is purposeful. The principle encompassed various aspects, including goal expression, goal pursuit, goal relationship, goal interaction, goal and discourse coherence, goal realisation means, goal realisation conditions, goal and power relationship, goal realisation, and goal and meaning (Liao, 2004b, 2005a, 2005b, 2005c, 2007, 2009a, 2009b, 2010, 2012a, 2013a). This principle holds 'that human verbal communication is goal-oriented or goal-driven and the process of communication is a process of pursuit of respective goal(s)' (Liao, 2009a: 62–63). It suggests that communication without a goal is meaningless, and that pursuing a goal is essential for effective communication (Liao, 2009a, 2009b).

To exemplify the application of his principle and verbal communication, Liao (2009b: 106–107) illustrated the process of pursuing goal(s) with authentic data taken from a court trial.

> Judge: In accordance with Articles 28 and 31 of the Criminal Procedure Law of the People's Republic of China, the defendant has the right to request the disqualification of members of the collegiate bench, court clerks, public prosecutors, and interpreters. Defendant Zhang, do you understand?
>
> . . .
>
> Judge: Defendant Mo, do you understand?
> Defendant: Yes, I understand.
> Judge: Have you made any requests for the disqualification of members of the collegiate bench, court clerks, or public prosecutors?
> Defendant: Thank you.
> Judge: Have you made any requests for disqualification?
> Defendant: Yes.
> Judge: Do you understand?
> Defendant: Yes, I understand.
> Judge: Have you made any requests for the disqualification of members of the collegiate bench, court clerks, or public prosecutors?
> Defendant: Yes, thank you.
> Judge: Defendant Mo, do you know what 'requesting disqualification' means?
> Defendant: I don't understand.
> Judge: You don't understand? Let this court explain it to you. Requesting disqualification means that if you believe that members of the collegiate bench, public prosecutors, or court clerks are relatives of the parties involved in the case, or have a close relationship with them, or if they serve as witnesses, defense attorneys, or legal representatives in this case, and their involvement could potentially affect the fair trial of this case, you have the right to request their disqualification. So, in your opinion, can the members of the collegiate bench, court clerks, and public prosecutors in this case conduct a fair trial? If you believe they cannot, you can request their disqualification. If you believe they can, you don't have to request disqualification. So, are you requesting disqualification or not? Will you request disqualification?
> Defendant: No, I am not requesting disqualification.

Liao argued that communication is often not completed or concluded with a single exchange of words, making it a process that is inherently complex.

In some communicative events, the ultimate outcome is success, but the process is filled with failures – from partial failures to eventual success. On the other hand, there are instances where the final outcome is failure, yet the process is not devoid of successes – from partial successes to eventual failure. And he finally concluded that the ultimate success or failure, as well as the complexity and twists of the process, are inseparably linked to the speaker's goals.

Over the past decade, Professor Liao and his fellow researchers have dedicated themselves to developing and refining this theory. They have published numerous papers exploring different dimensions of the Goal Principle, such as its relationship to discourse coherence, communicative patterns, contextual dynamism, speech acts, and context. Key works in this series include 'The Principle of Goal and Analysis of Discourse Coherence – A New Approach to the Study of Discourse Coherence' (Liao, 2005c), 'The Principle of Goal Direction and Goal Analysis' (Liao, 2009a, 2009b), 'The Principle of Goal and Dynamics of Context' (Liao, 2010), 'The Principle of Goal Direction and Interaction of Speech Acts' (Liao, 2012a), and 'The Principle of Goal and Contextual Studies: On Human Beings as the Key Factor of the Context' (Liao, 2013a). Additionally, other scholars have contributed to the field with works like 'An Analysis of the Purpose Relations in the Courtroom Discourse' (Zhang, 2010) and 'Interpretation and Application of the Pragmatic Goal Principle' (Huang & Wang, 2013). Interested readers can study the aforelisted' literature in depth.

In conclusion, the Principle of Goal has served as a foundation for understanding the purposeful nature of communication and its significance in achieving effective discourse. It has made valuable contributions to forensic linguistics and courtroom discourse analysis.

3.2.3 Functional Linguistics and Functional Forensic Discourse Analysis

As mentioned earlier, forensic linguistics in the West does not have its own theory and methods. Instead, it adopts theories and methods from various branches of linguistics, such as phonetics, lexicology, syntax, semantics, pragmatics, sociolinguistics, psycholinguistics, corpus linguistics, and computational linguistics, to analyse and study legal language and discourse. Coulthard et al. (2017: 121) metaphorically referred to these linguistic theories that linguists can select and use as a 'linguistic toolkit' in their seminal work. In recent years, this toolkit has been continuously updated with new tools, like the DIT and the Principle of Goal discussed in the last two sections, or the honing of existing tools, among which SFL is becoming an increasingly sharpened tool.

Halliday (1985, 1994) mentioned that functional grammar can be applied to legal practice, stating that it can 'assist in legal adjudications by matching samples of sound or wording'. This was a hot topic in the emerging field of forensic linguistics at that time, and it still is in current international forensic linguistics. It is the area of authorship analysis and speaker identification. However, few scholars in SFL have responded to Halliday's vision to explore legal language, except for Körner (2000), who conducted a doctoral dissertation on the evaluative language analysis of judgements in the common law system, which is a remarkable work in the application of SFL to legal language research. On the other hand, forensic linguists mostly favoured theories of phonetics, semantics, pragmatics, and sociolinguistics to analyse the 'idiolect' of speakers. Few people applied functional linguistic theories and methods to relevant research and practice, except for John Gibbons, who was one of the few forensic linguists adopting SFL.

Entering the new century, with increasing exposure, some forensic linguists have gradually realised the power of SFL and developed a growing interest in its theoretical framework (Heffer, 2007; Felton-Rosulek, 2009, 2015; Gales, 2010, 2011, 2015; Gales & Solan, 2017; Bartley, 2017, 2018, 2020, 2022). Notably, Nini and Grant (2013) first described two contrasting approaches to authorship analysis in forensic linguistics: the cognitive and the stylistic approaches. Then they proposed using aspects of SFL, such as Hasan's codal variation, to bridge the apparent differences between the two. This research strongly supported Coulthard's theory of idiolect, demonstrating that SFL is an effective theory for authorship attribution, bridging the gap between stylistic and cognitive approaches to authorship analysis. Hurt and Grant (2019) studied the evaluative language of pledging to harm, primarily analysing the differences in language expression between realised and unrealised violent fantasies. Hunter and Grant (2022) examined the relationship between attitudinal resources and psycho-pathological characteristics in writings by serial killers.

Aston University has been at the forefront of research into forensic linguistics and has found that it is no longer limited to the description of criminal discourse but is attempting to integrate language description with language services. The research by Hurt and Hunter aimed at providing linguistic clues for law enforce-ment in solving cases, in accordance with Coulthard's consistent advocacy and representations on the future direction of forensic linguistics. As Coulthard et al. (2017: 215) have stated, while many forensic linguists consider their work to be essentially descriptive, others believe that they are working within a 'critical discourse' framework. Their purpose is not merely to describe but to attempt remedies when problems are identified, actively serving the purposes of judicial practice, and promoting the realisation of fairness and justice.

In December 2016, the Martin Centre for Appliable Linguistics at Shanghai Jiao Tong University held an interdisciplinary international conference on SFL and forensic linguistics, inviting the SFL linguist James Martin and forensic linguists Edward Finegan, Gale Stygall, and Chris Heffer. At the symposium, Martin presented his discourse research on the practice of 'Youth Justice Conferencing' (YJC) that he conducted with Zappavigna and others. This research focused on an alternative judicial practice outside of court trials, namely the negotiation of dispositions for young offenders and the healing of victims through roundtable conferencing, embodying the concept of 'restorative justice'. Martin paid attention to the language and multimodal resources used by participants in such judicial practices. In addition to conducting exchange structure analysis, appraisal language analysis, and multimodal discourse analysis of the participants' language, Martin specifically focused on the concept of restorative justice underlying such judicial practices (Martin et al., 2012, 2013; Martin & Zappavigna, 2016). This line of research has broadened the scope of forensic linguistics.

Zappavigna and Martin (2018) summarised the advantages of YJC as follows:

1. Compared to traditional imprisonment, the conferencing format is more flexible and adaptable. The conference's content can be adjusted according to specific cases to achieve the desired outcomes.
2. The conferences provide an opportunity for victims to voice their concerns and have a direct impact on the outcomes of the case. This promotes a sense of empowerment and healing for the victims.
3. The conferencing format encourages dialogue and communication between all parties involved, fostering understanding and empathy.
4. Restorative justice aims to address the underlying causes of the offending behaviour, focusing on rehabilitation and reintegration rather than punishment.

This approach has positively reduced recidivism rates among young offenders (Martin & Zappavigna, 2016). However, the effectiveness of restorative justice, particularly regarding young offenders' genuine expression and engagement in the conferences, has been questioned. Some researchers have argued that there is a power imbalance in the conferences, with convenors exerting control over the discourse and young offenders feeling limited in their ability to express themselves authentically (Martin et al., 2013). This raises concerns about the true effectiveness of restorative justice practices in achieving its intended goals.

In China, the intersectional research between SFL and forensic linguistics is primarily conducted by Professor Yuan Chuanyou and his team at the GDUFS, and Professor Wang Zhenhua and his team at Shanghai Jiao Tong University.

This section will focus on Yuan's work, and Wang's contributions will be introduced in the next section.

Professor Yuan has long been engaged in integrating SFL with forensic linguistics for interdisciplinary research, which can be labelled as 'functional forensic discourse studies'. Before pursuing a doctoral degree in forensic linguistics, Yuan had extensively studied works and literature in functional linguistics, particularly Halliday's Systemic Functional Grammar, which laid the theoretical foundation for his doctoral research. During his doctoral studies under the supervision of Professor Du Jingbang, he was fortunately mentored by Professor John Gibbons, who was then working at Hong Kong Baptist University and had introduced Martin's recently proposed Appraisal System theory to him. Yuan applied this theory to the study of Chinese police interrogative discourse for his doctoral dissertation and published a monograph titled *Avoiding Revictimization: A Study of Police Interrogative Speech* (Yuan, 2010).

After completing his doctoral degree, he continued to draw upon new theories of functional linguistics and apply them to lawyer discourse (Yuan & Liao, 2010; Yuan & Hu, 2011), as well as analysing appraisal resources in prosecutor discourse (Yuan & Hu, 2012). In 2012, he was awarded a research grant from the National Social Science Foundation to study multimodal legal education discourse, with a particular focus on the study of anti-corruption discourse and the discourse of the rule of law (Liu, 2019a, 2019b; Yuan et al., 2021; Liu & Yuan, 2022). He has participated in numerous international conferences on forensic linguistics and SFL, presenting on the multimodal features of anti-corruption and rule of law discourse in China. Professor Yuan qualified as a doctoral supervisor in 2013 and since 2014 he has enrolled twelve doctoral students in forensic linguistics. They have used the theoretical underpinnings of SFL to address various issues in Legal and Forensic Linguistics, such as Liu (2019) on the multimodal construction of 'Rule of Law' in Chinese anti-corruption discourse, Tao (2018) on the discursive construction of presumption of innocence in legal news, Zheng (2019) on the discourse analysis of psychological correction in community corrections, Lu (2021) on the legal reasoning of judicial opinions, Wang (2023) on the genre of police interrogation discourse, Guo (2023) on the media reports of self-defence cases, and Luo (2023) on the tenor negotiation in community corrections discourse.

Professor Yuan's 'Community Corrections Discourse Studies in China' is a practical research project initiated in 2015 to align forensic linguistics research with social needs. Drawing on the practical experience and expertise of Martin and his team's research on YJC discourse in New South Wales, Australia, the project established the 'Community Corrections Discourse Research and Service Platform' in Guangzhou, which was jointly constructed by the GDUFS and the Guangzhou Bureau of Justice. Through this platform, a group of master's and doctoral students conducted in-depth fieldwork and research in judicial institutions and multiple community correction service agencies, working in collaboration with frontline judicial social workers, and collecting a large amount of valuable first-hand data. The team members used the theoretical frameworks of SFL to study the linguistic and multimodal discourse features of judicial social workers and probationers and submitted multiple research reports to the Bureau of Justice, which were endorsed by the bureau leadership. To date, the team members have completed more than ten master's theses and two doctoral dissertations and published multiple academic papers in domestic and international journals.

One of these projects, reported in Zheng and Yuan (2021), employed anthropological fieldwork and functional linguistic discourse analysis to analyse the discourse construction of the identity of judicial social workers. Based on the 'specialisation' dimension of Legitimation Code Theory, in conjunction with the Appraisal System, Zheng and Yuan proposed an analytical framework for the discursive construction of the identity of judicial social workers. The research showed that judicial social workers exhibit four identities in individual education conversations in community corrections: educators, managers, helpers, and coordinators. These four identities are constructed and reinforced by evaluative resources used by judicial social workers. Zheng and Yuan's article provided judicial social workers with discursive choices that are in line with their identities, thereby improving the accuracy and effectiveness of individual education conversations in community corrections, and optimising educational and correctional work. An earlier article by Zheng and Yuan (2018) published in a law journal explored the multimodal discourse construction of the defendant's identity in community corrections. Zheng (2019) also studied how supervisors use language and body language in their individual semantic repertoire to construct their own identities to influence the court's judgement on the application of community correction for offenders.

Luo and Yuan (2019) studied the discourse of initial assessment in community corrections from the perspective of functional linguistic exchange structure, with the aim to reveal the exchange structure patterns and existing problems of social worker discourse, in order to provide social workers with more effective discourse choices and ideal discourse exchange structure models, and thus to improve the accuracy and effectiveness of the initial assessment. Yuan and Luo (2021) also probed deeper into the two exchange structures of risk assessment discourse in community corrections: K1^(K2 f) and K2^K1 patterns. Their research showed that judicial social workers need to enhance their language awareness, and probationers need more effective language choices to improve the accuracy and effectiveness of risk assessment. Further research results from this project were the doctoral dissertations by Zheng (2019) and Luo (2023), and additional research papers are expected in the near future. Hopefully, these will be of practical use in guiding the discourse practice of community corrections and contributing to the overall improvement of community corrections.

In addition to the research outcomes produced by this project, other research topics are of equal significance in terms of theoretical innovation and practical value. For instance, Lu (2021) examined, from a genre perspective, the discursive construction of legal reasoning in the high-quality judicial opinions of the US Supreme Court, addressing research questions regarding how legal reasoning is constructed through particulate, periodic, and prosodic structures, and offering a useful reference for Chinese judicial reform regarding judgements writing related to their legal reasoning. Guo (2023) studied the evaluation of media reports on self-defence cases, revealing the active role played by new media in disseminating the concept of justifiable defence and ingraining the ideology that 'the law shall not compromise with lawlessness' in people's minds. It is an excellent doctoral dissertation, which was highly praised by the doctoral defence committee and Professor Martin, who mentored her while she was a visiting student at the University of Sydney.

During his tenure as the third President of the CAFL (2018–2022), Professor Yuan has engaged in promoting the development of forensic linguistics in China and collaborating with international forensic linguists by working as an Ordinary Member of the Executive Committee of the IAFL (2013–2017) and attending seven successive biennial conferences of the IAFL since 2009.

Through the efforts of Yuan and his colleagues, GDUFS successfully obtained the hosting rights for the 12th Biennial Conference on Forensic Linguistics in 2013 and successfully organised a remarkable conference, known as IAFL12 in 2015, receiving high praise from the international legal linguistics community.

IAFL12 was characterised by several notable 'firsts': it was the first time that IAFL held its biennial meetings in an Asian country, with an unprecedented scale, numerous expert invitations, intensive exchanges, and interactions between domestic and international scholars, and a wealth of academic content. It was the first time the conference walked into a Chinese court, allowing participants to observe a trial of an international case in China's courtroom and listen to speeches by Chinese judges, providing insights into the evolution and reforms of China's judicial system. This facilitated frequent exchange and integration between academia and the judicial community, promoting mutual understanding. It was the first time the conference was interviewed and featured on a provincial television station, with a televised interview program broadcast globally. This academic interview program, titled FACETIME, introduced the field of legal linguistics to audiences worldwide. Furthermore, the university's leadership attached great importance to the conference, with the then president, Zhong Weihe, meeting the then president of the association, Edward Finegan, at the earliest convenience and expressing strong support from the university. Chen Jianping, the then deputy secretary of the university's party committee, delivered a welcome speech, while Vice President Liu Jianda attended the welcome banquet and delivered a speech. Vice President Shi Youqi, a professor of law, delivered a keynote speech at the conference, introducing China's path to legal construction, with a focus on the important concept of 'rule of law' from the Fourth Plenary Session of the 18th Central Committee, providing a refreshing perspective for domestic and international scholars.

In addition, the conference showcased another highlight by presenting local theories and research from GDUFS. This allowed the world to gain a better understanding of Professor Du Jinbang's 'Theory of Legal Discourse Information' and Professor Yuan Chuanyou's research in the new field of 'multimodal public legal discourse', meanwhile demonstrating GDUFS's strength in legal translation and courtroom interpreting, as well as the outstanding research potential of the doctoral and master's students.

3.2.4 Legal Discourse as a Social Process

Professor Wang Zhenhua is the executive director of the Martin Centre for Appliable Linguistics, which was set up at Shanghai Jiao Tong University in 2013 with the aim of fostering the dialectic of theory and practice that Halliday had envisioned as 'appliable linguistics'. The Centre's principal research foci include academic discourse, forensic linguistics, language typology, translation studies, and corpus linguistics. This research has been highlighted in a dedicated forum focusing on one of these areas each year. Since its inception, it has organised two international events on forensic linguistics, one being the *International Conference on Appliable Linguistics and Legal Discourse* held in 2016, and the most recent *Symposium on Appliable Linguistics and Legal Discourse* held jointly by the Martin Centre and the CAFL in 2023. The two academic events greatly enhanced the development of forensic linguistics in China. At these events, there were presentations by

- Edward Finegan, on Deposition Testimony by Expert Linguists in US Civil Litigation: A Challenging Genre
- Janet Ainsworth, on Linguistic Issues in the Law of Product Safety Warnings: How Linguistic Research Could Improve the Law's Response to Dangerous Consumer Products
- Monwabisi K. Ralarala, on Transpreters' Translations of Complainants' Narratives as Evidence: Whose Version Goes to Court

- Wang Zhenhua, on 'Human-Speech-Action': As a Complex That Everyone Finds Hard to Walk Away With
- Yuan Chuanyou, on the Intersection between Functional Linguistics and Forensic Linguistics: The Functional Linguistic Approach to the Concepts of 'Rule-by-Law' and 'Rule of Law'.

Professor Wang Zhenhua has made tremendous and indelible contributions. Wang studied at the University of Sydney, where he was mentored by Professor Martin, a renowned expert in SFL. During his time in Sydney, he was exposed to Martin's Appraisal System and introduced it to China at an early stage (Wang, 2001). While studying in Sydney, he also came into contact with Australian forensic linguists such as Professors John Gibbons and Michael Walsh, who sparked his interest in forensic linguistics. He asked friends in China to send him Pan Qingyun's *Legal Linguistics* and Wang Jie's *Legal Language Research*, which greatly influenced him and led him onto the path of studying Legal and Forensic Linguistics. For many years, he has been committed to the integration of SFL and forensic linguistics, using functional linguistic theories and methods, particularly discourse semantics, as tools to analyse legal discourse/texts.

Professor Wang's research on forensic linguistics, particularly his central ideas on 'legal discourse as a social process', is embodied in a series of papers funded by the Humanities and Social Sciences Research Innovation Project of Shanghai Jiao Tong University ('Legal Discourse as a Social Process: A Perspective of Discourse Semantics'). These papers applied Martin's discourse semantics theory to study different types of legal discourse, including legislative language and judicial discourse. The discourse semantics theory was initially proposed by Martin in 1992 and further developed and refined through collaboration with Rose in 2003 and 2007. This theory inherits Halliday's classic SFL theory and elevates the study of systemic functions from the lexical-grammatical layer to the discourse semantics layer, focusing on constructing various semantic resources for discourse. The theory proposed six major systems at the discourse semantics level: negotiation, appraisal, ideation, conjunction, identification, and periodicity.

In this series of papers, Professor Wang and his co-authors defined social processes as the interactive process of people constantly making rational or irrational choices, establishing social relationships, forming alliances, and creating different factions and groups during their participation in social activities (Wang & Tian, 2017). Social processes were categorised into competition, conflict, adaptation, cooperation, and assimilation. The competition, conflict, adaptation, cooperation, and assimilation experienced by individuals within a legal context are often constructed in discourse and instantiated as various types of legal discourse. In other words, legal discourse is an instantiation of highly generalised social process types within a legal context. Through the analysis of appraisal, negotiation, identification, conjunction, periodicity, and ideation, this series of papers comprehensively examines the process of meaning presentation (ideational metafunctional perspective), meaning negotiation (interpersonal metafunctional perspective), and meaning weaving (textual metafunctional perspective) in legal discourse. Conflict, competition, adaptation, cooperation, and assimilation are realised in the process of meaning presentation, negotiation, and weaving. Language users achieve these social processes by making appropriate choices among the choices available in the six discourse semantic systems already mentioned.

The first paper in this series, Wang and Liu (2014), provided a preliminary exploration of the concept of 'legal discourse as a social process'. This paper adopted the framework of individuation and Appraisal theory within SFL to investigate the operational mechanisms of constructing social relationships through the individuation of discourse meanings from the perspective of attitude bond and interpersonal harmony in discourse semantics. The research showed that the process of individuation and constructing attitudes is the process of constructing interpersonal relationships. When attitudes are constructed by different individuals conflict, it may lead to interpersonal conflict. On the other hand, when attitudes tend to converge among different individuals, it is easier to achieve interpersonal harmony. Harmonious interpersonal relationships can be built by selecting appropriate discoursal resources, constructing and sharing attitudes, and establishing attitude bonds.

In the second paper of the series, Wang and Zhang (2015) further explicated the viewpoint of Legal Discourse as a Social Process, considering Legal Discourse as a Social Process formed by competition, conflict, compliance, cooperation, and assimilation. Guided by the theories of SFL, particularly Martin's genre theory, the paper utilised the periodicity and identification systems at the discourse level as the analytical framework for studying the semantic organisation of legal discourse. It explored the five social processes in legal discourse and the patterns in which they are realised. The analysis revealed that legislative discourse pursues structural simplicity at the discourse level, while judicial discourse, especially oral discourse such as cross-examination, tends to be complex and subjective. These characteristics are closely related to the different social process goals to be achieved by different types of legal discourse.

The third and fourth papers in the series respectively studied legislative discourse and judicial discourse as social processes. Wang and Wang (2016) selected the Marriage Law of the People's Republic of China as an example to explore the realisation of the five social processes of competition, conflict, compliance, cooperation, and assimilation in the legislative discourse from the perspective of ideational semantics (ideation system and conjunction system). They discussed how legal discourse regulates social processes and ultimately promotes social harmony through ideational semantics. The paper pointed out that as a social process, legal discourse regulates people's choices, mediates competition, resolves conflicts, promotes compliance, cooperation, and assimilation, and ultimately achieves social harmony. Tian and Wang (2016) analysed the distribution of attitude resources in Chinese criminal defence speeches, considering legal discourse in a competitive social process, carrying a significant interpersonal semantics load. The paper examined the distributional characteristics of attitude resources from the perspective of the Appraisal System and found that the most used attitude resource is Judgement, followed by Appreciation and Affect. The paper argued that Judgement is a mandatory resource in the argumentation section, while Appreciation and/or Affect are optional.

Wang's theory of 'legal discourse as a social process' was further developed in the fifth paper by Wang and Tian (2017), forming a discourse semantic view within the framework of SFL. The paper categorised social processes into differentiation-type and integration-type social processes. Differentiation-type social processes include competition and conflict, while integration-type social processes include compliance, cooperation, and assimilation. The paper then interpreted Legal Discourse as a Social Process from the perspective of the social semiotic view of SFL. In this process, there is competition, conflict, compliance, cooperation, and assimilation among legal subjects. The supervenient view of context and discourse semantics is employed to construct a research path to address the formation and realisation of these processes. The former functions as the theoretical scaffolding, and the latter provides specific analytic toolkits. It is argued that the study of Legal Discourse as a Social Process should not only consider the contextual constraints but also the meaning choice. Only in this way can people's manipulation of legal discourses to realise communicative goals and intentions be comprehensively and thoroughly revealed.

In summary, within the paradigm of SFL, this series of five papers explored the realisation of competition, conflict, compliance, cooperation, and assimilation as social processes in legal discourse from six discourse semantic systems. They investigated how legal discourse achieves different social processes through semantic selection under the constraints (or influences) of social contexts, providing a research perspective of discourse semantics for the study of legal discourse and making significant contributions to Chinese forensic linguistics.

Wang Zhenhua has recently shifted his focus to the multimodal analysis of courtroom discourse. In this line of research, Li and Wang (2019) reviewed the relevant achievements in multimodal research on legal discourse and raised the three main topics in this field: the study of multimodal functions, the study of multimodal interaction, and the study of multimodal critical discourse analysis in legal discourse. The authors explored the problems and solutions regarding the theoretical foundation, research methods, and research perspectives in this field. Finally, the article combined the application of digital technology in judicial practice and provided an outlook on future research in this field. Zhao and Wang (2022) focused on the interactivity between language and gesture in the context of lawyer identity construction by adopting the theoretical framework of the language/gesture composite communication system (Goldin-Meadow & McNeill, 1999) and paralanguage system (Martin & Zappavigna, 2019). They proposed an analytical framework for constructing lawyer identity through observation and discourse semantic analysis. The research results showed that lawyers use language and paralanguage to construct three types of identities in court: expressers of litigation attitudes, maintainers of litigation positions, and enhancers of litigation viewpoints, and that the results suggested practical significance for the analysis and positioning of lawyer identity. Finally, Qu and Wang (2022) focused on the multimodality of conflict negotiation discourse. Drawing on the theoretical essence of SFL and social semiotics, they proposed a multimodal design framework for conflict negotiation discourse and applied it to analysing civil litigation cases in China. This framework integrated the analysis of the context, semantics, and lexicogrammar of conflict negotiation discourse and incorporated the process and rationale of multimodal discourse design. It added a multimodal feature analysis to the language negotiation framework and highlighted the subjectivity of symbol users. This study aimed to inspire more multimodal research on conflict negotiation and explored the design concepts from the perspectives of linguistics and semiotics, providing insights into the practice of conflict negotiation.

Wang Zhenhua has made significant contributions to the field of forensic linguistics, particularly in his notion of 'legal discourse as a social process' and his research in the area of multimodal analysis of courtroom discourse. His contributions have prepared the way for further research and have practical implications for the analysis and positioning of lawyer identity in forensic linguistics.

3.2.5 Empirical Studies on Language Evidence

As mentioned in the Introduction of this Element, China's evidence law system has been imperfect. For a long time, the provisions on expert witnesses have been missing until recently when they were written into the Civil Procedure

Law in the capacity of 'persons with specialised knowledge' or 'people with expertise' to act as 'expert supporters' or 'expert assistants' in court, but there is no mention of linguistic experts as people with expertise; therefore, it is extremely rare for them to testify in court or give expert opinions. Despite these difficulties, there have been some attempts by legal and forensic linguists to contribute to offering language evidence in real cases. A case in point is *Yang* v. *Hu*, a reputation infringement case involving language evidence.

A young actress, Hu Xiaoqiong (the defendant and appellant), met a director named Yang Yichao (the plaintiff and respondent) in late 2005 and sought a role in a drama directed by Yang, with whom she was in contact over dinner and text messages. In August 2006, Hu was not cast in the drama. Then Hu opened a blog on Sina (a Chinese social media/blog platform), publishing articles that alleged that Yang had used his position as director to ask Hu to drink with him on several occasions, and that he had sent her sexually suggestive messages, asking her to have sex with him as a condition for her casting. After Hu refused, Yang retracted his promise. In her articles, Hu lashed out at this 'subterfuge' between actresses and male directors in the entertainment industry. Yang issued a statement accusing Hu of slander, to which she continued to respond with articles and interviews with journalists accusing Yang of shamelessness and hypocrisy. Yang also spoke to journalists, accusing Hu of speculating for ulterior motives, and later took the case to court because she had infringed his right to reputation. The trial court asked Hu to prove the content of her articles. She submitted to the court as evidence the text messages between Yang and her from the communications company.

The text message evidence between Hu and Yang reads (translated) as follows.

(1) Hu: You've been busy lately, right?
(2) Yang: Yes, I've been busy, but it doesn't stop me from thinking about you!
(3) Hu: Haha, then one day when you are free to come out and get together.
(4) Yang: I don't want to go out, I want you to come in!
(5) Hu: That's too profound! I am too stupid to understand it!
(6) Yang: Haha, then you don't understand.
(7) Hu: Is your play still on for August 15th?
(8) Yang: Of course, it's not kidding!
(9) Hu: Oh that's good! Do I have any hope of working with you?
(10) Yang: How can we work together if you don't come in?
(11) Hu: I am rather obtuse, what do you mean by 'coming in'?
(12) Yang: Think about it, it's easy!
(13) Hu: It's hard to think! Why don't you just tell me directly?
(14) Yang: Just come to my 'thinking' and let my 'wanting' come to life!

Neither party disputes the truthfulness of the content. Hu argued that the words were sexually suggestive. Yang argued that this was his flirtatious language used as a poet, that 'wanting you to come in' was a way to get Hu to bring money into the production, and that 'my "wanting"' was synonymous with this.

The trial court (Beijing Dongcheng District People's Court) held that the content mentioned was truthful text. However, from the perspective of the general public perception of society, the language of the plaintiff is too intimate, as well as obscure, and may cause ambiguity. But this was not enough to find that the plaintiff issued a sexual innuendo to the defendant. The defendant was found liable for an infringement of the libel law. It was decided that Hu should delete the infringing articles, apologise to Yang, and pay compensation of 10,000 yuan for moral damages. Then Hu appealed to the Beijing No. 2 Intermediate People's Court, which held that Hu had failed to provide substantive evidence of the content of her articles. The content of the aforementioned text messages, which were verified to be true, was not sufficient to conclude that Yang had made sexual advances to Hu. The Court dismissed Hu's appeal and upheld the trial court's verdict.

After the initial trial, Hu commissioned the Legal Language Research Centre of China University of Political Science and Law to conduct a 'semantic identification' of whether the text messages were sexually suggestive. The 'linguistic evidence analysis' made by three experts from the said Centre states that 'a man saying, "I miss you" to a woman of his age or younger than himself is no longer a thought in the usual sense, but a 'want' with a special desire for the opposite sex, especially when coupled with an intimate title such as "dear"'. The 'verbal seduction' is evident. In response to Yang's interpretation of 'come in' as bringing in funds, the analysis notes that

> such a matter needs to be expressed directly and clearly. With Hu explicitly stating, 'I don't understand', Yang should have explained himself clearly, yet he did not. Although a man has emotional desires, as a man of status and position and who has mastered certain language skills, some desires are not appropriate to be spoken out directly, so he has to refrain from explaining them.

The opinion points to 'let my "wanting" come to life' as a further sexual innuendo, and 'It is the hidden nature of Yang's communicative purpose in language that leads him to express it through the linguistic means of suggestion.' The conclusion is that there was 'sexual innuendo' in Yang's verbal solicitation of Hu. Although commissioned by Hu, this opinion is not neutral but still represents an opinion. Hu submitted the opinion as language evidence to the appellate court but it was not admitted by the court.

In June 2007, at the *First National Seminar on Analysis, Authentication and Judicial Application of Language Evidence*, chaired by Professor Wang Jie, Director of the Centre, a group of legal language scholars and forensic linguists presented papers on the text message evidence in the *Yang* v. *Hu* reputation infringement case. The scholars each used relevant theories of linguistics and communication, such as contextual analysis, discourse analysis, implication analysis, and ambiguity analysis, to analyse the text message evidence. They came to the same conclusion: that the text messages do contain 'sexual innuendo'.

Based on this case, several academic papers have discussed text messages as language evidence. Lou (2007) analysed two pieces of verbal evidence in this case by applying knowledge of linguistics (lexicography, semantics, stylistics, and rhetoric) and communication (speech communication and mass communication) and concluded that (1) in the first instance, the plaintiff's mobile phone text message to the defendant was sexually suggestive; and (2) in the petition for appeal, the defence's argument that 'weblogs (blogs)' are the same as traditional logs is inaccurate. Instead, the defendant's blog is of the nature of mass communication. In another paper, Zou (2008) advocated the concept of language evidence and its semantic examination. She first classified the types of language evidence and deemed the text messages in the case to be valid. She then introduced semantic examination as a linguistic method to examine the contents of the language evidence, including the identification of its nature and purpose. She further conducted a semantic analysis of the language evidence by employing Grice's Conversational Implicature theory and Speech Act theory to show how disparate interpretations of the language evidence have become the critical cause for judicial disputes. She finally called for judges to consult linguists' analyses of language evidence, and for a rational and proper judge to guarantee judicial fairness and improve judicial public credibility. The paper by Zhang (2007) focused on the contextual factors, such as time, relationship, and power difference between the disputants in interpreting the text evidence itself. Zhang proposed a contextual analysis of linguistic evidence in the hope that it could be a reference for interpreting such linguistic evidence. Wei (2008), taking this case as an example, further explored the issue of the burden of proof for the truth of facts of infringing statements in reputation cases, the paradox in the burden of proof, the standard of proof of evidence, and the question of how to give support to just and critical statements in reputation cases by questioning certain issues in the trial and judgement of this case. Wang (2011) also made a detailed speech-chain or turn-taking analysis of the text messages and found that they did contain 'sexual innuendo'.

Zhang and Wang's (2022) study of the normalisation of expert opinion based on linguistic evidence demonstrated that an expert support person is often confused with the roles of a lawyer, expert, and witness. This confusion of roles has created a unique dual system of expert supporters and appraisers, with the effect that the opinions provided by expert supporters are considered to lack legal validity and are generally not adopted by judges as the basis for deciding cases. This study touched on the dilemma that arises with the adoption of expert supporters' opinions as the object of research, focusing on the court trial process, and analysing the reasons for this dilemma and confusion, and possible ways to avoid them. In analysing the expert opinion on linguistic evidence in the case of *Beijing Qihu Technology Co. Ltd.* v. *Wang Xiaochuan*, Zhang and Wang's paper focused on the meanings of 'regret' and its Chinese translations, and discussed how to regulate expert opinions and what position expert supporters should adopt in a trial.

Cheng and Wang (2017) introduced the linguistic evidence and expert testimony practised in common law jurisdictions, particularly in the United States. They considered its implications for the newly introduced 'person with expertise' in the revised Civil Procedure Law and Criminal Procedure Law in China, which allowed 'the person with expertise' to appear in court and render expert opinions. The paper explored civil and criminal cases tried by the federal courts of the United States from four perspectives: manifestations of 'linguistics evidence', qualifications to proffer expert testimony, analytical methods adopted by expert witnesses, and judges' standards and discretions on linguistic evidence. The authors finally drew implications that '[T]hough there is a disparity in systems of law and rules of evidence between the PRC and the United States, the comparatively mature judicial experience of the United States is still able to enlighten the future orientation of the quasi-counterpart ("person with expertise") in the judicial practices of the PRC.' (Cheng & Wang, 2017: 196).

3.2.6 Legal Translation and Interpreting Studies

Legal translation and interpreting, described as 'an act of communication in the mechanism of law' (Šarčević, 1997: 3–4), has played a crucial role in facilitating cross-language, cross-jurisdiction, and cross-cultural communication in China (Xu & Yu, 2023). Its significance has become even more pronounced as China endeavours to share stories about its legal system with the world. Taking a comprehensive perspective, Xu and Yu (2023) thoroughly examined the advancements in legal translation and interpreting in China, exploring its role in modernising the Chinese legal system, promoting legal exchanges, and fostering mutual understanding of legal cultures. They discussed recent findings related to theoretical principles and frameworks of legal translation, the protection of language rights for ethnic minorities and foreigners in court, and efforts to standardise legal translation and interpreting practices. In this section, we will first provide an overview of the main research topics in the field of legal translation, offering a comprehensive understanding of the current status quo. Subsequently, we will present the DIT-based theoretical exploration of legal translation and interpreting in China.

1. Main research topics

When searching for '法律翻译' (legal translation) on https://www.cnki.net/, the official website of China National Knowledge Infrastructure (CNKI), which is a platform integrating significant Chinese knowledge-based information resources, we found that as of 20 April 2023, 153 Chinese papers were published in Chinese Social Sciences Citation Index (CSSCI) journals covering twenty major research topics. Table 1 demonstrates that these papers primarily concentrate on four main areas: legal texts and translation (Topics 4, 8, 13, and 20), translation of legal terminology (Topics 2, 16, and 17), translation of legislative texts (Topics 11, 12, 14, and 15), and the development of legal translators (Topics 6, 9, and 19).

(1) Studies on legal texts and translation

As a kind of 'professional discourse' (Bhatia, 1993), legal texts could be classified into three categories based on their functions, that is, purely prescriptive (such as laws, contracts, and wills), purely descriptive (such as scholarly legal works and

Table 1 Major topics of study on legal translation in China.

Topics	
1. Legal translation (61)	11. The Civil Code(4)
2. Legal terminology (10)	12. Legislative texts (4)
3. Legal English (10)	13. Translation of legal texts (4)
4. Legal texts (8)	14. People's Republic of China (4)
5. Legal language (6)	15. Civil Code of the People's
6. Legal translators (5)	Republic of China (4)
7. Legal English translation (5)	16. Principle of identity (3)
8. Translation strategies (5)	17. Translation of terms(3)
9. Translation teaching (4)	18. Law in ancient China(3)
10. Legal transplantation (4)	19. Cultivation of translators (3)
	20. Legal discourse (3)

legal reports), and partially prescriptive and partially descriptive (such as judgements) (Šarčević, 1997: 11). Zhang (2001: 192) highlighted the importance of analysing the typological features of legal texts prior to translation. He contended that in so doing, the legal translator could grasp the global intention and function of the texts. Besides, the legal translator could set the appropriate translation criteria and choose the translation techniques accordingly.

Hence, before translation, it is vital to study the typological features of legal texts. For example, based on studies on the 'de' structure that is frequently used to introduce a condition in legislation (Sun & Zhou, 1997), Lin and Ji (2002) explored ways to translate the 'de' structure and propose that we may adopt English sentence patterns like Whoever . . . / Anyone who . . . / No one who . . . / Where . . . or add a concrete subject instead. Likewise, based on features of legislative and judicial texts, Li and Zhang (2005) put forward six practical principles of legal translation: accuracy and precision, consistency and identity, clarity and concision, professionalism, standardised language, and teamwork. The first two principles are related to the faithfulness of translation, the second one to the expressiveness of the target texts, and the last one to the professionalism required in legal translation.

(2) Studies on the translation of legal terminology

Due to differences in languages, legal systems, and legal–cultural traditions, problems with the asymmetry and incongruity of legal terms pose great challenges for legal translators (Ramos, 2021). Hence, scholars are keen on the discussion of equivalence of legal terms. Du (2005) advanced three principles to deal with near-equivalent, partial equivalent, or non-equivalent legal terms, including the principle of language deferring to the law, the principle of tolerance for difference and pursuit of concord, and the principle of imitation and complement. Cheng, Sin, and Cheng (2014) claimed that to achieve equivalence, legal translators are also involved in a process of socio-semiotic and cultural mediation. Similarly, based on bilingual law drafting in the Hong Kong Special Administrative Region, Chan (2020) argued that to achieve terminological equivalence, we could create legal Chinese that 'naturally accommodates common law concepts and statutes from the English legal system and to reconcile Chinese legal terms from the different legal systems adopted by Hong Kong, Mainland China, and Taiwan'.

In addition to equivalence, efforts are also made to keep consistency in translating legal terms. The National Legislative Affairs Office compiled a booklet on legal terms to standardise the translation of laws and regulations at the national level (Qu, 2012). Regrettably, the booklet was not open to the public and failed to be updated in time. As a result, inconsistency of legal terms still exists in legal translation. For example, it has been found that the legal term '依法治国' is translated into different expressions, such as 'exercising the rule of law', 'rule/govern the country by law', 'run state affairs according to law', and 'law-based governance' (Zhao & Xue, 2023: 25). Hence, the principle of consistency and identity (Li & Zhang, 2005) should be carefully observed, and a national standard for legal translation and a term base for legal terms are urgently needed.

(3) Studies on the translation of legislative texts

Unlike countries or regions where English is one of the official languages and the English version of the law is equally authentic, the translated English version of laws and regulations in China is not authentic. Should there be any discrepancy between the Chinese and English versions, the Chinese version is deemed to prevail. Nevertheless, there have been unfailing efforts to translate legislative texts into other languages, particularly English. This kind of translation enthusiasm could largely be attributed to underlying needs, such as attracting foreign investment, promoting legal exchanges, and offering litigation or non-litigation legal services (Qu, 2022).

Academic interest in translating legislative texts peaked when the English version of the Civil Code of the People's Republic of China was released in 2020. Zhang (2021) focused on the translation process of the Civil Code, regarding it as a grand systematic translation project. Taking the core terms in the property rights section of the Civil Code as an example, Zhao and Xue (2022) compared the concepts related to property rights in Chinese, German, and Japanese with the intention of finding ways to solve the problem of non-equivalence arising out of legal transplantation.

(4) Cultivation of legal translators

Under the 'Belt and Road' initiative, China has been engaged in deeper cooperation with neighbouring countries. As a result, the cultivation of legal translators has become an urgent task for China in the new era (Zhang, 2018). However, there are still many problems in China regarding formal education at school. For instance, there are insufficient teaching hours and a shortage of competent teachers who are good at both theory and practice in translation (Xu, 2017).

Great efforts have been made to tackle the problem. In 2007, the Ministry of Education decided to set up the Master of Translation and Interpreting (MTI) programs that particularly aim to bring up professional translators through two-year master's degree education. In 2008, the GDUFS took the lead in training legal translators. However, statistics showed that only a tiny portion of students work as legal translators upon graduation, which is surprisingly incompatible with the original mission of the MTI program (Ma, 2017). Zhao (2018) argued that in order to train competent legal translators, it is necessary to make legal translation an independent discipline so that we can accurately set the goal, systematically design the curriculum, and properly choose teaching modes.

2. The DIT-based studies on legal translation and interpreting

Apart from fruitful research findings from the four topics introduced in last section, recent years have also witnessed prominent theoretical progression on legal translation and interpreting in China. For example, given the insufficiency of existing translation strategies, such as dynamic equivalence on legal translation, Li (2010) put forward the principle of static equivalence. The principle of static equivalence caters to unique linguistic features and special functions of legal texts, including 'the static nature of legal language informative nature of the translated versions stereotyped writing style rigidity of translation criteria and the restricted readership of legal documents' (Li, 2010: 59). Creative as the principle is, there are few studies to develop the principle of static equivalence.

On the contrary, the DIT-based exploration of legal translation has demonstrated great vitality and has been widely applied to contrastive analysis of discourse features of the source and target texts, court interpreting, and assessment of translation quality.

The Information Bridges Framework in Contrastive Legal Discourse Analysis (Zhao, 2011) offers a theoretical framework for legal translators to carefully examine the discourse features of the source and target texts. Drawing on insights from cross-cultural communication, comparative studies, and discourse information, this framework outlines four information bridges that need to be bridged during legal translation: the sociocultural system, linguistic conventions, the legal system, and the stances and attitudes of discourse users. The four information bridges are interrelated with each other. In addition to attending to linguistic differences, legal translators also need to deal with other information issues before a particular word or phrase is chosen.

Unlike legal translation, where legal translators could ponder over the sentence and easily deal with the information gap, court interpreters are expected to decide in a hair-splitting way. As a result, it has become important to examine whether important information is lost or distorted. Tian (2008) analysed the changes in information elements in the courtroom and summarised three types of information element changes: information loss, information enrichment, and information reorganisation.

While it is natural to reorganise information during interpreting, legal translators and interpreters should be cautious with information loss or addition. Any minor change in the original information or how information is presented may deviate from the source text. As a result, it is important to assess the translation quality based on information exchanged in legal translation (Du, 2014: 362). The DIT-based quality assessment framework for legal translation (Du, 2012) consists of three assessment levels: the information, technical, and artistic levels. The macroanalysis and microanalysis of information is used to assess whether the translation faithfully conveys the content of the source text. At the macro level, we may find out whether the target text preserves the generic features of the source texts by comparing their information tree structures. At the micro level, we may compare information elements. Based on the performance of the target texts at the information level, we may further assess the expressiveness and elegance of the texts by examining strategies used by the legal translator.

Preliminary as the assessment framework may be, it provides a new perspective to assess the quality of legal translation. It has been found that it is helpful to apply information elements in legal translation teaching, where students are more sensitive to information exchange and have improved the accuracy of legal translation (Du, 2010). More theoretical and empirical DIT-based studies on legal translation are needed and will be carried out in the future.

4 Prospects in the 2020s and Beyond

This section will explore prospects for the future of Legal and Forensic Linguistics in China. It begins by addressing the naming issues within the discipline and then offers an outlook on various emerging research topics under the new name, including cyberbullying language, Internet court discourse analysis, authorship analysis and expert assistance systems, and speaker identification and forensic phonetics.

4.1 Naming Issues of the Discipline

Forensic linguistics, as mentioned earlier in this Element, has a rich history dating back to the late 1960s. The term was first introduced by Svartvik in 1968 and later popularised by Coulthard in the early 1990s. This led to the establishment of IAFL, the official journal *Forensic Linguistics*, and the organisation of *Biennial Conferences of IAFL*.

As the field of forensic linguistics expanded, scholars began to question the narrow focus of the term 'forensic'. They argued that it did not fully encompass the breadth of the discipline, which includes the analysis of linguistic evidence in court, as well as the study of legal language, legislative language, and communication barriers within the legal system.

To address these concerns, Peter Tiersma, the late former president of the association, played a significant role in renaming the association's journal to *The International Journal of Speech, Language and the Law* (IJSLL). He also proposed a similar name change for the association itself, but the members voted against it. Tiersma went on to establish the *International Language and Law Association* (ILLA) as a separate organisation.

After decades of debate, the Association established a 'Naming Subcommittee' to consider a possible name change. The subcommittee conducted extensive research and consultation and recommended a new name: *The International Association for Forensic and Legal Linguistics*. This new name reflects the addition of 'legal linguistics' to broaden the scope of the association's work and the change from 'linguists' to 'linguistics' to emphasise a common area of interest.

During the consultation process, differing views emerged. Some suggested using 'Language and Law' instead of 'Forensic Linguistics', while others defended 'Forensic Linguistics' for its inclusion of investigative activities and evidence presentation in court. Ultimately, the membership voted in favour of the name change.

The resolution was reached at the 15th Biennial Conference of the Association (IAFL15) held at Aston University in September 2021, and the Association's name was officially changed to *The International Association for Forensic and Legal Linguistics*. This new name recognises the distinction between the narrow and broad interpretations of forensic linguistics. It encompasses the analysis of linguistic evidence in courts as well as the study of legal language, legislative language, and communication barriers within the legal system.

The name change signifies the evolution and inclusiveness of the discipline, attracting professionals and researchers from various backgrounds. It highlights the association's commitment to advancing knowledge and promoting international cooperation.

In conclusion, the name change reflects the expansion and diversity of the field. It acknowledges the interdisciplinary nature of forensic and legal linguistics and fosters collaboration among researchers and practitioners from diverse backgrounds. By adopting this new name, the Association aims to create a more inclusive and comprehensive framework for the discipline, embracing both the narrow and broad aspects of forensic linguistics. This change represents a significant milestone in the field of forensic and legal linguistics, fostering collaboration, advancing knowledge, and promoting the exchange of ideas among professionals dedicated to the study of language and law.

In China, the discipline of forensic linguistics has also faced controversy regarding its name, and different names are still used in academic circles. Some scholars prefer to use terms like 'legal linguistics' (法律语言学, Falv Yuyanxue), 'judicial linguistics' (司法语言学, Sifa Yuyanxue), 'courtroom linguistics' (法庭语言学, Fating Yuyanxue), 'investigative linguistics' (侦查 语言学, Zhencha Yuyanxue), and so on. However, there is a consensus among academics that Chinese forensic linguistics has always been a study of legal language in its broad sense, rather than a narrow focus on linguistic evidence, due to the country's civil law legal system and the absence of rules on linguistic evidence and expert witnesses in the law of evidence. Zou (2018) argued that further consideration and construction are needed for the disciplinary name and connotation of legal linguistics as an interdisciplinary field between law and linguistics. She emphasised that legal linguistics, studying 'legal language' as its object, can be generally or partially considered as 'legal' linguistics, while forensic linguistics is more focused on applying linguistic and linguistic-philosophical theories and methods to law and jurisprudence.

Prominent figures in the field of legal language studies in China, including Chen Jiong, Pan Qingyun, and Wang Jie, are primarily scholars involved in teaching and researching Chinese in political and law schools. Their focus lies in exploring the rhetoric and practical application of language in Chinese legal contexts, offering valuable insights into the use of legal language to the law-makers, the judiciary, and the law enforcement. While they rarely employ the term forensic linguistics, Chen Jiong advocated for establishing legal or forensic linguistics as early as 1985. On the other hand, foreign language legal linguistic researchers, such as Du Jinbang, Liao Meizhen, and Yuan Chuanyou, have introduced forensic linguistics and its theories and research methods from abroad to analyse language use within local legal contexts. However, their primary emphasis is examining language in judicial activities and documents, such as police interrogations, courtroom discourse, and judgements. They seldom delve into the study of linguistic evidence in court or engage in expert testimony as part of judicial practice. Although they accept the term forensic linguistics, they typically translate it into Chinese as 'legal linguistics' in a broader sense, rather than the narrower sense of 'forensic linguistics'. Wu Weiping has used both 'forensic linguistics' (1994) and 'language and law' (2002a) interchangeably. As Professor Pan Qingyun suggests (personal communication), there is no need to impose uniformity in naming conventions. Therefore, the name change of the *International Association of Forensic and Legal Linguistics* seems to have minimal impact on the discipline's name in China, and there is no need to change the Chinese name, which remains as '法律 语言学' (Falv Yuyanxue). However, regarding the English name, the term 'legal and forensic linguistics" ' may be more suitable for China. Consequently, in alignment with the international association's name change, it was proposed to modify the name of the domestic association from *China Association for Forensic Linguistics* to *China Association for Legal and Forensic Linguistics*), or *China Association for Forensic and Legal Linguistics*.

4.2 Outlook of Legal and Forensic Linguistics in China

Young Chinese Legal and Forensic Linguistics scholars have recently probed some new research fields, such as Xu Youping's cyberbullying language and Internet court discourse studies, Zhang Shaomin's authorship analysis, and Cao Honglin's speaker identification or authentication.

4.2.1 Cyberbullying Language Research

Cyberbullying, also known as cyber harassment or online bullying, has emerged as a significant global social issue. Referred to as the first pandemic of the twenty-first century (Jacobs, 2020), cyberbullying has inflicted detrimental physical and psychological effects on its victims, including anxiety, depression, and suicidal ideation (Hinduja et al., 2008; Klomek et al., 2010; Sampasa-Kanyinga et al., 2014; Miller &Kimberly, 2017).

Cyberbullying is commonly defined as 'an aggressive and intentional act perpetrated by an individual or group, utilising electronic means of communication, repeatedly and over time, against a victim who may struggle to defend themselves' (Smith et al., 2008). Key defining properties of cyberbullying include intent, repetition, power imbalance, direct and indirect forms of bullying, and the perception of the victim (Ira-Katharina & Petermann, 2018).

While young students are commonly perceived as the most vulnerable targets of cyberbullying, adults can also fall victim to online harassment. For instance, in July 2022, a girl with pink hair faced relentless cyberbullying after sharing a video online in which she joyfully announced her acceptance into a prestigious master's program while her grandfather lay in a hospital bed. Hurtful comments like 'good girls don't dye their hair pink' and 'pink hair is not suitable for serious girls' haunted her, ultimately leading to her tragic suicide six months later.

Previous studies on cyberbullying have predominantly approached the issue from sociological, psychological, and computer science perspectives, focusing on its nature, detection, and prevention, while paying limited attention to the linguistic aspects of cyberbullying. However, language, acting as an 'invisible fist' in cyberbullying, serves as vital evidence for identifying, combating, and regulating such behaviour (Xu, 2020). Examining one of the most high-profile cyberbullying incidents in China, Xu (2020) analysed the linguistic features on a weblog. In addition to negative adjectives, Xu observed the use of nouns like 'beast' and pronouns such as 'it', which are typically employed to describe animals, being applied to describe the victims of cyberbullying. Considering the context-sensitive nature of cyberbullying language, greater attention should be directed towards implicit linguistic expressions and linguistic patterns that could serve as indicators for detecting cyberbullying.

Drawing on the context model proposed by van Dijk (2008), Xu (2024) analysed the various roles assumed by participants in cyberbullying, based on data collected from three litigated cyberbullying cases in China. She highlighted that seemingly disconnected posts and comments online are interconnected within the cyberbullying discourse. Therefore, carefully examining the textual relationships between posts and comments can provide insights into participant interactions and assist courts in attributing responsibilities to bullies and their supporters based on their roles in the cyberbullying dynamic.

In addition to studies on the features of cyberbullying acts and participant roles, there are also investigations into the intentions of perpetrators in cyberbullying. Zhang (2020) examined flaming language on the social media site WeChat in China, which may incite crimes or moral wrongs. In order to reveal the flaming nature of WeChat accounts, this paper analysed twenty-six suspect articles from a Chinese WeChat subscription account from the perspectives of corpus linguistics and pragmatics. This paper found that linguistic clues to flaming (cyberbullying) could be recognised and revealed in terms of keywords, semantic prosodies, and speech acts. It also discovered that the language crime of incitement requires only the inciter's illocutionary act, that is, intention, rather than the outcome of the incitement, and that the perpetrator's intentions heavily influence the speech act of inciting hatred.

Despite the widespread occurrence of cyberbullying globally, very few cases result in legal action. One of the main challenges is the lack of relevant laws and regulations to address this issue. Recognising this problem, many countries have taken steps to enact legislation specifically targeting cyberbullying. For instance, in the United States, nearly every state has either introduced new sections or amended existing laws to combat cyberbullying. In China, a new article was added to the Law of the People's Republic of China on the Protection of Minors in 2020. This article explicitly prohibits organisations or individuals from insulting, slandering, threatening, or engaging in other cyberbullying acts against minors through various forms of online communication, including text, images, audio, and videos (Article 77). However, it is unfortunate that this article only mentions the option for parents to report cyberbullying incidents to the platform and request the removal of offending content.

While one option to tackle cyberbullying is to filter out offensive words by creating blacklists, it is essential to note that seemingly neutral words and phrases can be used in a derogatory manner within specific contexts. Therefore, collaborative efforts are necessary to decipher the linguistic features that define cyberbullying, establish and update flexible blacklists, and identify effective linguistic parameters for detecting cyberbullying (Xu & Trzaskawka, 2021). Only through such efforts can future studies on automated cyberbullying detection and legislative measures regarding cyberbullying become more practical and effective.

4.2.2 Internet Court Discourse Analysis

The rapid advancement of the information age, particularly the integration of Internet technology and the justice system, has sparked a global interest in digitising justice. Various 'Internet Plus' trial modes have been developed to leverage Internet technology in streamlining litigation activities. Examples include online mediation programs in Singapore (Cole & Blankly, 2006) and video link testimonies in Canada (Gluzman, 2018). In 2017, the Hangzhou Internet Court was established, followed by the Beijing Internet Court and Guangzhou Internet Court in 2018, making them the world's first batch of Internet courts (Zhou, 2017).

Adhering to the principle of 'handling online disputes online', Internet courts in China handle cases related to the Internet within their jurisdiction. They provide a comprehensive online dispute resolution service, ensuring that the entire process, from case filing and evidence examination to hearings, mediation, adjudication, and judgement enforcement, is conducted online. Consequently, Internet courts are tasked with exploring new avenues for cyber governance and innovating judicial practices in the information era (Zhou, 2017).

Internet courts have introduced several new modes of litigation, such as combined online trials, demonstrative online trials, and asynchronous trials (Jing, 2022). These trial modes offer advantages such as reducing judicial costs, improving efficiency, and enhancing accessibility to justice. However, as pioneers in cyber justice, Internet courts in China face numerous challenges. For instance, when justice is conducted online (Du, 2016), it remains questionable whether litigants have a better opportunity to express their true needs and have their voices heard and emotions felt in Internet courts (Sung, 2020).

Preliminary linguistic studies have been conducted to uncover the dynamics within Internet courts in China. From a semiotic perspective, Zheng and Wang (2021) compared the physical courtroom with the cyber courtroom in terms of visual elements and layout. They found that traditional semiotic resources in physical courtrooms, such as the elevated bench and face-to-face arrangement of litigants' tables, are marginalised or even replaced by new visual elements and patterns in Internet courts. Consequently, the traditional sense of authority, legitimacy, rationality, and hierarchy associated with physical courtroom settings may diminish. In contrast, the online courtroom's fresh image contributed to perceptions of accessibility, openness, and equality in Internet courts.

Similarly, Xu (2024) explored the (de)construction of judges' identities in Internet courts from a semiotic perspective. She examined how judges' traditional centralised identity is semiotically deconstructed, while new identities, such as troubleshooters and procedural adjustors, are constructed. Her data analysis revealed that judges' centralised dominating identity is jointly deconstructed by a variety of semiotic resources, including the decentralised lineal display of judges' image on the screen, various background images of parties that introduce daily discourse into the institutional one, and parties' interruptions, questions, and suggestions. However, her analysis also found that the use of inclusive 'we' and flexible change of speakers depict judges' concerns, understanding, and tolerance for parties, implicitly constructing judges' new identities as troubleshooters and procedural adjustors.

Empowered by technologies like big data, cloud computing, artificial intelligence, and blockchain, Internet courts are continuously innovating litigation processes and judicial operations in the information era. As an increasing number of unrepresented litigants appear online in Internet courts, it becomes crucial to study how judges can guide lay participants through online litigation without sacrificing efficiency (Xu, 2021). The impact of new technologies on the justice system is unavoidable (Jing, 2022). Therefore, it is important to conduct linguistic analyses of Internet court discourse and explore how 'justice for all' can be linguistically realised online in smart courts.

By delving into the linguistic aspects of Internet court discourse, researchers can gain insights into online justice's unique features and challenges. Semiotic analyses, as demonstrated by Zheng and Wang (2021) and Xu (2024), shed light on the visual and symbolic representations within Internet courts, revealing shifts in power dynamics and the construction of new judicial identities. These studies highlight the potential for significant changes in the digital realm's perception and experience of justice.

Furthermore, linguistic analyses can help identify potential issues and areas for improvement within Internet court proceedings. For example, the question of whether litigants can effectively express their needs and have their voices heard in online settings remains a concern (Sung, 2020). Examining the linguistic interactions and discourse patterns can provide valuable insights into how communication dynamics may impact the fairness and effectiveness of Internet court proceedings.

Additionally, linguistic analyses can contribute to developing guidelines and best practices for Internet court proceedings. By examining language use, including inclusive pronouns and flexible speaker roles, judges can better understand and address the parties' needs, facilitating a more collaborative and supportive environment.

4.2.3 Authorship Analysis and Expert Assistance System in China

Authorship analysis serves the purpose of identifying the author of a given text (authorship identification) or providing demographic or psychological group features of the author of an anonymous text to narrow down the scope of the investigation (authorship profiling). The concept of idiolect, which refers to a distinct and individual version of the language, enables authorship analysis by manifesting itself through unique and idiosyncratic choices in texts (Coulthard, 2004: 432). However, it is important to note that detecting consistency and determining distinctiveness requires a substantial and diverse body of text before these idiolect features become noticeable or measurable (Grant, 2021: 559).

Authorship analysis has been extensively utilised in various cases in common law countries. Forensic linguists are often called upon to provide expert opinions based on their observations of the frequency or rarity of specific linguistic features in the texts under examination (Coulthard, 2021: 529). Two distinct methodologies, namely the cognitive and stylistic approaches (Grant, 2022), are commonly employed in authorship analysis, with forensic stylistics being a widely used technique that utilises linguistic analysis of writing style for authorship identification (McMenamin, 2021: 539), despite certain limitations.

However, in China, expert opinions on legal language are not admissible in court. Nevertheless, there have been court rulings on plagiarism in literary and translated works where authorship analysis could have played a significant role. One such case is the *Qiong Yao* v. *Yu Zheng* (2015) copyright infringement case. In this instance, the plaintiff, Qiong Yao, a renowned writer, accused Yu Zheng, a well-known director, of plagiarism. To support her claim, the plaintiff enlisted the assistance of Wang Hailin, an experienced screenwriter, as an expert assistant to provide opinions on whether the disputed script involved plagiarism. These expert opinions were incorporated into the main text of the court judgement, ultimately contributing to the plaintiff's victory.

A more recent case occurred in 2023, where a man in China was brutally killed and preserved in a refrigerator by his wife (the defendant) for over fifteen months. Astonishingly, even after the victim's death, the defendant continued to send messages to his parents and update his social media accounts, and no one suspected anything unusual. In a further twist, the defendant later deceived the victim's parents of 200,000 yuan. Amidst public outrage over the defendant's heartless actions, a pressing question arises: if ordinary citizens possessed even a basic understanding of authorship and were attuned to idiolect, how might the outcome have differed? At the very least, the victim's parents could have detected abnormal messages, alerted the authorities much earlier, and potentially avoided financial losses.

While expert opinions on legal language are not currently admissible in Chinese courts, research interest in authorship analysis has never stopped. For instance, Zhang (2020) conducted a study exploring methods for identifying authors of short texts by examining features in pragmatics, discourse semantics, and discourse information for authorship attribution in Chinese microblogs. The study utilised a set of twenty-eight microblogs written by four authors, each contributing seven articles. Experimental, textual analysis, and statistical methods were employed to test and attribute all possible eleven combinations of the four authors. The findings reveal that five distinct combinations of values extracted from the fields of pragmatics, discourse semantics, and discourse information were able to significantly differentiate all eleven discriminative combinations of the four authors. Consequently, it was concluded that these extracted features in pragmatics, discourse semantics, and discourse information could effectively distinguish microblogs authored by different individuals, with a discrimination accuracy rate ranging from 85.7 per cent to 100 per cent. Based on these results, the text-based classifier for the four authors demonstrated statistical validity and applicability to authorship attribution in other types of Chinese short texts.

Discourse Information Theory presents a fresh perspective in the realm of authorship analysis. Drawing upon the DIT, young scholars have begun to analyse the stylistic features of short messages, literary works, and anonymous tip-off letters from the standpoint of discourse information (Luo, 2012; Cui, 2013; Xiong, 2016; Zhang, 2020). They aim to identify discourse information features that could serve as parameters in authorship analysis. This approach opens new avenues for exploring the relationship between language use and authorship.

Future studies in this field could focus on assessing the reliability of discourse information parameters in authorship analysis and consider incorporating the Likelihood Ratio technique in drawing conclusions. In recent years, scholars like Zhang Shaomin have utilised experimental methods to simulate language evidence within legal contexts and have achieved some success in analysing suspicious text authors. It is hoped that her research, along with other endeavours, will garner recognition and attention from the legal community, further advancing the field of authorship analysis.

In the field of authorship analysis, expert opinions play a crucial role in litigation, especially when dealing with complex and specialised issues that are beyond the knowledge of judges, lawyers, and the parties involved. In China, the legal system allows for the engagement of expert assistants, sometimes referred to as Chinese 'expert witnesses', to provide opinions on professional matters and strengthen the persuasiveness of the parties' arguments. Although the rules regarding expert assistants need further improvement, they can still be utilised effectively in authorship analysis.

In China, 'persons with specialised knowledge' are considered a distinct category of litigation participants. Unlike ordinary witnesses, these individuals possess expertise in specific professional areas and are called upon to make statements in court. However, it is important to note that their opinions are treated as statements from the parties rather than traditional witness testimonies. The costs associated with their appearance in court are borne by the parties who request their involvement. As a result, they do not possess the same level of neutrality as expert witnesses in common law systems.

In the United States, expert witnesses are permitted to provide opinions or other forms of testimony to assist the fact-finder in understanding scientific, technical, or specialised evidence. Similarly, in England and Australia, expert witnesses have specific duties to the court that supersede their obligations to the parties involved in the litigation process. In China, the system of persons with specialised knowledge, also known as expert assistants, was first established in 2001 and subsequently elevated to the level of basic law in civil litigation. The highest judicial authorities have clarified that the role of expert assistants is to assist the parties by providing opinions on specialised issues or cross-examining expert opinions. They do not serve as 'professional assistants' to the judge and are distinct from the court's expert appraisers. This positioning allows the parties to enhance their litigation capabilities by utilising the expertise of professionals in their favour.

Currently, in China, there has been a significant increase in the number of experts testifying in court, particularly in fields such as forensic pathology, forensic clinical identification, forensic psychiatry, DNA identification, handwriting identification, seal identification, and writing formation time identification, but not in the field of forensic authorship analysis. China's civil and criminal procedural laws have incorporated elements of the expert witness system from European and American legal systems, allowing for the presence of expert supporters or expert assistants. These legal provisions enable the cross-examination of expert opinions by expert witnesses. For example,

Article 82 of the Civil Procedure Law allows parties to request the appearance of a person with specialised knowledge to provide an opinion on expert opinions or professional issues. Similarly, Article 197 of the Criminal Procedure Law grants the same right to the public prosecutor, parties, defence, and litigation agents to call upon a person with specialised knowledge to provide an opinion on appraisal opinions made by experts.

The presence of expert assistants in court proceedings has greatly facilitated the development of domestic judicial experts testifying in court. Provisions such as Articles 83 and 84 of the Several Provisions of the Supreme People's Court on Evidence in Civil Proceedings (2019) outline the process for applying for the appearance of a person with specialised knowledge. Written applications containing the relevant information and purpose of the application must be submitted to the court. The court has the discretion to grant or deny the application. Once granted, the person with expertise appears in court, and the judge has the authority to question them.

In conclusion, utilising expert assistants or persons with specialised knowledge has become integral to the Chinese legal system. While forensic linguistics is not recognised as specialised knowledge, and forensic authorship analysis is not admissible, we are confident in improving the rules and regulations pertaining to linguists as expert assistants. Their involvement can significantly strengthen the parties' arguments and enhance their litigation capabilities. The presence of linguistic expert assistants contributes to a more comprehensive and effective authorship analysis process in China's legal proceedings, and this is also supported by their ability to provide opinions and cross-examine expert testimonies.

4.2.4 Speaker Identification and Evidence of Forensic Phonetics in China

Speaker identification, considered more 'scientific' than authorship analysis and expert opinions, is highly recognised by law. Scholars in China have been translating the works of Western researchers and conducting domestic research in the Chinese legal context.

Jessen et al. (2010) provided an overview of forensic phonetics, with a focus on speaker identification as its core task. Speaker profiling and classification are used when the offender has been recorded but no suspect has been found. Auditory speaker identification becomes relevant when no speech recording of the offender is available. It can involve familiar-speaker identification or unfamiliar-speaker identification, and in the latter case, a voice line-up or voice parade can be conducted. When recordings of both the offender and a suspect are available, an expert in forensic speech analysis performs a voice comparison. Research issues and domains in voice comparison analysis include the Bayesian approach, the Likelihood Ratio, formant frequency measurements, non-analytic perception, Exemplar Theory, forensic automatic speaker identification, and the interaction between different methods.

Wang et al. (2012) introduced the concept of the voiceprint, which refers to the image of speech analysed and displayed through spectrograms. It is metaphorically referred to as voiceprint in forensic science, resembling fingerprints. Voiceprint now refers to the collection of sound characteristics that serve as evidence in litigation. Voiceprint identification is an interdisciplinary field that applies knowledge from linguistics, phonetics, physiology, psychology, physics, computer science, and statistics. It involves comparing and analysing auditory and spectral features of evidence sounds with known sounds to determine if they originate from the same source. It also involves comprehensive analysis to determine the nature or source of the sound. This specialised technical method provides evidence for judicial activities and clues for investigative activities.

French et al. (2019) reviewed developments in forensic speaker comparison in the UK, highlighting milestones and changes in methodology, conclusion frameworks, regulation of forensic phoneticians, and the development of reference databases. Forensic voice comparison, also known as voiceprint or speaker identification, typically involves comparing and identifying speech and speech patterns in criminal recordings with known suspect recordings.

In China, voiceprint identification can be broadly or narrowly defined. In the narrow sense, it refers to speaker identification or forensic voice comparison. Due to differences in terminology between domestic and international judicial practices, the term '声纹鉴定' (voiceprint identification) is widely used in China instead of a literal translation of the original term 'forensic speaker comparison'. The major research in this area is summarised in Table 2.

Cao Honglin, an expert appraiser, has been involved in court appearances related to voiceprint and image/video identification. He has contributed to the field with his expertise and has been recognised for his work. He is currently leading a research project to investigate the development of domestic voice identification.

In summary, speaker identification and evidence of forensic phonetics play a significant role in the Chinese legal context. Scholars and experts are actively researching and applying these techniques in courts, providing valuable evidence for judicial activities, and contributing to the development of the field.

Table 2 Major research studies on voiceprint identification in China.

Study	Details
Cao and Lei (2017)	• Forensic speaker comparison, focusing on evaluating the similarity between samples and the typicality of features in the relevant population. • Provides statistics for the fundamental frequency (F0) of young Chinese male speakers, which can be used as reference data in forensic speaker comparison casework.
Cao and Ding (2018)	• Empirical study on applying forensic phonetics evidence in courts across major cities in China. • Analysed various variables such as forensic institute, cause of action, case nature, recording methods, and expert opinions to explore the practical problems and application of forensic phonetics evidence.
Cao and Zhang (2020)	• The present status of forensic phonetics evidence in courts across all provinces in China. • Survey analysed variables such as caseload, forensic institute, cause of action, recording methods, and expert witness appearances, providing a comprehensive overview of the application of forensic phonetics evidence in China.

5 Conclusion

In this Element, we have explored the fascinating journey of forensic linguistics in China, tracing its origins, documenting its progress, and examining its prospects. The Element highlighted the significant contributions of scholars and researchers who have played a pivotal role in shaping and advancing the field. The origins of forensic linguistics in China can be traced back to the 1980s and 1990s. During this period, legal language studies by Chinese language and legal scholars laid the foundation for the discipline. Proposals were made to establish legal linguistics as a discipline, leading to its formal establishment. As legal language studies gained momentum, scholars recognised the need for a specialised field that focuses on analysing language evidence in legal contexts. This led to the introduction of forensic linguistics into China by foreign language researchers who brought their expertise and experiences to enrich the field.

Forensic linguistics in the 2000s witnessed remarkable advancements in language and law studies. Scholars such as Professor Pan Qingyun and Professor Wang Jie made significant contributions to the field, expanding the understanding of language and discourse in legal contexts. Professor Pan Qingyun's research on legal language and communication contributed to developing methodologies for analysing legal language. Professor Wang Jie's work on legal discourse analysis and legal interpretation shed light on the complexities of language in legal settings. Their contributions provided valuable insights into the linguistic aspects of legal cases and the role of language in the legal system.

Theoretically, the development of forensic linguistics in China was influenced by the work of Professor Du Jinbang and his DIT. Professor Du's research focused on the analysis of discourse structures and the extraction of information from language. His work on DIT provided a theoretical framework for analysing legal language and contributed to understanding how discourse can reveal crucial information in legal cases. Furthermore, Professor Liao Meizhen's research on the Principle of Goal expanded the understanding of language use in legal contexts. The Principle of Goal emphasised the communicative goals of legal actors and their impact on the language used in legal discourse. This research not only deepened the understanding of legal language but also highlighted the importance of considering legal actors' communicative goals and intentions.

The application of functional linguistics in the Functional Forensic Discourse Analysis conducted by Professor Yuan Chuanyou and his team further enhanced the understanding of language use in legal settings, particularly in the context of community correction. Systemic functional linguistics focuses on the functions and meaning-making of language in context, and its application in forensic linguistics allowed for a deeper analysis of the meaning and intent behind language use in legal contexts. Functional Forensic Discourse Analysis examines the meaning-making strategies employed in legal discourse and how they contribute to the construction of legal arguments and the resolution of legal disputes. This approach provides valuable insights into the persuasive strategies used in legal communication and the impact of language choices on legal outcomes.

The exploration of Legal Discourse as a Social Process, carried out by Professor Wang Zhenhua and his team, also contributed to the development of forensic linguistics in China. Understanding Legal Discourse as a Social Process involves examining the interactions between legal actors, the power dynamics at play, and the social process, which involves competition, conflict, adaptation, cooperation, and assimilation. This research shed light on how language is used to negotiate legal meanings, establish authority, and construct legal identities. It enhanced the understanding of legal discourse by contextualising it within the broader socio-legal framework.

Empirical studies on language evidence have also significantly advanced forensic linguistics in China. Empirical studies examined real-life legal cases and language data to identify patterns and characteristics that can be used as evidence in the trial of the cases. This empirical approach strengthened the scientific basis of forensic linguistics and provided objective evidence that can withstand scrutiny in legal proceedings. Additionally, legal translation and interpreting studies addressed the challenges and complexities of translating legal texts and interpreting legal discourse accurately, playing a crucial role in facilitating cross-language, cross-jurisdiction, and cross-cultural communication in China.

Looking towards the future, the Element discussed the prospects of Legal and Forensic Linguistics in China. One of the key aspects discussed is the naming issues within the discipline. As forensic linguistics continues to evolve and gain recognition, it is important to establish an unambiguous name that accurately reflects its scope and purpose within the Chinese context. A well-defined name will enhance the visibility and understanding of forensic linguistics and facilitate its integration into the legal system.

Furthermore, the Element explored emerging research areas that hold great promise for the future of forensic linguistics in China. Cyberbullying language research is an important area of study, considering the increasing prevalence of online communication and its potential legal implications. Cyberbullying, including online harassment or online bullying, has emerged as a significant global social issue, posing significant challenges in terms of identifying perpetrators, understanding the impact on victims, and implementing appropriate legal measures. Understanding the linguistic features used in cyberbullying cases can aid in identifying perpetrators and implementing effective legal measures to address online harassment and protect victims.

Another area of research highlighted in the Element is the semiotic and linguistic analysis of the Internet court discourse. With the rise of online dispute resolution platforms and the establishment of Internet courts, analysing the language used in online legal proceedings becomes crucial. Online communication presents unique language use, comprehension, and interpretation challenges. Analysing the language used in Internet court proceedings can enhance the efficiency and fairness of online dispute resolution processes. It can also shed light on the linguistic dynamics of online legal communication and provide insights into how language choices impact the resolution of legal disputes in the digital age.

Authorship analysis and expert assistance systems were also discussed as promising research areas. The ability to accurately determine the authorship of texts, particularly in cases involving anonymous or disputed documents, can provide valuable evidence in legal investigations. Authorship analysis involves examining linguistic features, writing styles, and textual patterns to identify the author of a particular document. Developing expert assistance systems that utilise linguistic analysis can further support legal professionals in their decision-making processes. Forensic authorship analysis can help identify relevant linguistic patterns and assist in drawing conclusions in legal cases. By leveraging technological advancements and linguistic expertise, authorship analysis and expert assistance systems have the potential to revolutionise the field of forensic linguistics and enhance the efficiency and accuracy of language analysis in legal proceedings.

Additionally, the Element explored the field of speaker identification and evidence of forensic phonetics in China. Speaker identification plays a vital role in criminal investigations by matching recorded voices to potential suspects. Forensic phonetics, which focuses on analysing acoustic and auditory features of speech, provides the scientific basis for speaker identification. The Element highlighted the research and advancements made in speaker identification in China, including using voiceprints and spectrographic analysis. Speaker identification research in China contributes to developing robust methodologies that can withstand scrutiny in the legal system and provide reliable evidence for identifying speakers.

In conclusion, this Element presented a comprehensive and insightful exploration of forensic linguistics in China, tracing the historical origins of the discipline and highlighting the contributions of early scholars and researchers who laid the foundation for its development. The progress made in the 2000s was examined, showcasing the advancements in language and law studies and the significant contributions of renowned scholars. The Element also explored the prospects of Legal and Forensic Linguistics in China, addressing naming issues and identifying emerging research areas that hold promise for the future.

As a comprehensive overview of the field, this Element constitutes a valuable resource for scholars, researchers, and practitioners interested in forensic linguistics in China. It deepens the understanding of language evidence in legal contexts and highlights the interdisciplinary nature of forensic linguistics, drawing from disciplines such as linguistics, law, sociology, and technology. The contributions of Chinese scholars and researchers in advancing the field have been acknowledged, showcasing their expertise and the unique insights they bring to forensic linguistics.

References

Ainsworth, J. (2020). *The uses of theory in forensic linguistics: A plea for methodological cross-fertilization.* Keynote presentation at the 11th national conference of China's Association of Forensic Linguistics (CAFL11), Shanghai, China.

Atkinson, J. M. & Drew, P. (1979). *Order in Court: The Organization of Verbal Interaction in Judicial Settings.* London:Macmillan.

Bartley, L. (2017). *Transitivity, No Stone Left Unturned: Introducing Flexibility and Granularity into the Framework for the Analysis of Courtroom Discourse.* Unpublished PhD thesis, University of Granada.

Bartley, L. (2018). Justice demands that you find this man not guilty: A transitivity analysis of the closing arguments of a rape case that resulted in a wrongful conviction. *International Journal of Applied Linguistics*, *28*: 480–495.

Bartley, L. (2020). Please make your verdict speak the truth: Insights from an appraisal analysis of the closing arguments from a rape trial. *Text & Talk*, *40* (4): 421–442.

Bartley, L. (2022). A transitivity-based exploration of a wrongful conviction for arson and murder: The case of Kristine Bunch. *Language, Context and Text, 4* (2): 304–334.

Bennett, W. L. & Feldman, M. S. (1981). *Reconstructing Reality in the Courtroom.* New Brunswick, N. J.: Rutgers University Press.

Berk-Seligson, S. (1990). Bilingual court proceedings: The role of the court interpreter. In J. N. Levi and A. G. Walker, (eds.), *Language in the Judicial Process* (pp. 155–202). New York: Plenum Press.

Bhatia, V. K. (1993). *Analysing Genre: Language Use in Professional Settings.* London: Longman.

Boulle, L. (2005). *Mediation: Principles, Process, Practice (2nd ed).* Chatswood: LexisNexis Butterworths.

Braddock, R. (1958). An extension of the Lasswell Formula. *Journal of Communication, 8*(2): 88–93.

Büring, D. (1999). Focus and topic in a complex model of discourse. In G. Krifka & van der Sandt (eds.), *Focus and Presupposition in a Multi-speaker Discourse.* ESSLI-99 Workshop Reader. Utrecht: Utrecht University.

Cao, H. & Lei, Y. (2017). Fundamental frequency statistics for young male speakers of Mandarin. *Journal of Forensic Science and Medicine, 3*(4): 217–222.

Cao, H. & Ding, T. (2018). An empirical study on the application of evidence of forensic phonetics in courts of Beijing, Shanghai, Guangzhou, Shenzhen, Tianjin and Chongqing in China. *Evidence Science, 26*(5): 622–638.

Cao, H. & Zhang, X. (2020). An empirical study on the present status of the application of evidence of forensic phonetics in courts of China. *Chinese Journal of Phonetics, 8*(1): 90–104.

Chan, C. (2020). *Legal Translation and Bilingual Law Drafting in Hong Kong: Challenges and Interactions in Chinese Regions*. New York: Routledge.

Charrow, R. P. & Charrow, V. (1979). Making legal language understandable: A psycholinguistic study of jury instructions. *Columbia Law Review.* 79: 1306–1374.

Chen, J. (1985a). Legal linguistics should be established. *Modern Jurisprudence* (formerly *Law Quarterly*), 7(1): 77.

Chen, J. (1985b). Explorations in legal linguistics. *Journal of Anhui University, 26*(1): 49–52.

Chen, J. (1998). *Introduction to Legal Linguistics*. Xi'an: Shaanxi Education Press.

Chen, J. (2004). A review of legal language research in China over the past twenty years. *Journal of Bijie Normal College, 22*(1): 1–4.

Chen, J. (2011). The reconstruction of Prosecution-Defense-Judge relationship in China: A frame analysis of judges' discourse information processing. *International Journal of Speech, Language and the Law, 18*(2): 309–313.

Cheng, L., Sin, K., & Cheng, W. (2014). Legal translation: A sociosemiotic approach. *Semiotica, 2014*(201): 17–33.

Cheng, L. & Wang, J. (2008). A tudy on linguistic evidence. *Forensic Linguistics Study, 2*(2): 71–75.

Cheng, L. & Wang, X. (2017). Linguistic evidence and expert testimony: A study of admissibility in the field of judicial practice in the United States and its implications. *Journal of Zhejiang University (Humanities and Social Sciences), 47*(6): 181–196.

China News Network (2022, 4 November). *Cyberspace Administration of China: Strengthen the governance of cyberbullying!* China News Network. https://mp.weixin.qq.com/s/7FMqsI-RZmnjYw96StUQhQ.

China Internet Network Information Center (2022, 31 August). 2022/6 50th Statistical Report Basic Data. www.cnnic.net.cn/n4/2022/0916/c132-10593.html.

Cole, S. R. & Blankley, K. M. (2006). Online mediation: Where we have been, where we are now, and where we should be. *University of Toledo Law Review, 39*(38): 193–205.

Conley, J. M. & O' Barr, W. M. (1998). *Just Words*. Chicago: University of Chicago Press.

Coulthard, M. (1994). On the use of corpora in the analysis of forensic texts. *Forensic Linguistics*, *1*(1): 27–43.

Coulthard, M. (2004). Author identification, idiolect, and linguistic uniqueness. *Applied Linguistics*, *25*: 432–447.

Coulthard, M. (2021). In my opinion. In M. Coulthard, A. May & R. Sousa-Silva (eds.), *The Routledge Handbook of Forensic Linguistics* (pp. 523–538). Oxon: Routledge.

Coulthard, M. & Johnson, A. (2007). *An Introduction to Forensic Linguistics: Language in Evidence*. New York: Routledge.

Coulthard, M., Johnson, A. & Wright, D. (2017). *An Introduction to Forensic Linguistics: Language in Evidence (2nd ed.)*. London: Routledge.

Cui, S. (2013). *DIA Based Chinese Fraudulent Mobile Short Message (SMS) Detection*. MA thesis. Guangdong University of Foreign Studies.

Du, B. (2016). Staging justice: Courtroom semiotics and the judicial ideology in China. *International Journal for the Semiotics of Law*, *29*(3): 595–614.

Du, J. (2000). The macrostructure of forensic linguistics: An overview based on current research. *Modern Foreign Languages*, *23*(1): 99–107.

Du, J. (2004). *Forensic Linguistics*. Shanghai: Shanghai Foreign Language Education Press.

Du, J. (2005). Principles of legal exchange and legal translation. *Journal of Guangdong University of Foreign Studies*, *16*(4): 11–14.

Du, J. (2007). A study of the tree information structure of legal discourse. *Modern Foreign Languages*, *30*(1): 40–49, 109.

Du, J. (2009). A study on discourse information features of written exercise by English major students. *Foreign Language Teaching*, *30*(2): 42–46,56.

Du, J. (2010). The application of discourse information element analysis in the teaching of advanced legal translation. In Yu, S. (ed.), *Legal Language and Translation* (pp. 1–10). Shanghai: Shanghai Translation.

Du, J. (2011). Discourse information analysis: A new approach to forensic linguistics. *Journal of Social Science in China*, 15 (190).

Du, J. (2012, May 31-June 2). *A study on assessment of legal translation quality: From the perspective of discourse information*. 2nd International Conference on Law, Translation and Culture, The Hong Kong Polytechnic University, Hong Kong.

Du, J. (2013). *Tutorial on Discourse Analysis*. Wuhan: Wuhan University Press.

Du, J. (2014). *Legal Discourse Information Analysis*. Beijing: People's Publishing House.

Du, J. (2022). *Information Mining of Legal Discourse*. Beijing: Science Press.

Du, J. (2022). *On Discourse Information Mining*. Beijing: Science Press.

Du, J & Yu, S., eds. (2007). *New Progress in Legal Language Research*. Beijing: University of International Business and Economics Press.

Du, J., Chen, J. & Yu, S., eds. (2010). *Prospects of Forensic Linguistics in China*. Beijing: University of International Business and Economics Press.

Du, J. & Ge, Y. (2016). *On Methodology of Forensic Linguistics*. Beijing: People's Publishing House.

Eades, D. (1994). A case of communicative clash: Aboriginal English and the legal system. In J. Gibbons (ed.), *Language and Law* (pp. 234–264). Harlow: Longman.

Eades, D. (1995). *Language in Evidence: Issues Confronting Aboriginal and Multicultural Australia*. Sydney: University of New South Wales Press.

Eades, D. (1998). The Fields of Law and Language. *Forensic Linguistics: The International Journal of Speech, Language and the Law, 5*(2): 215.

Eagleson, R. (1994). Forensic analysis of personal written texts: A case study. In J. Gibbons (ed.), *Language and Law* (pp. 363–373). Harlow: Longman.

Felton-Rosulek, L. (2009). *The Sociolinguistic Construction of Reality in the Closing Arguments of Criminal Trials*. Unpublished PhD thesis, University of Illinois at Urbana-Champaign.

Felton-Rosulek, L. (2015). *Dueling Discourses: The Construction of Reality in Closing Arguments*. New York: Oxford University Press.

French, P., Cao, H. & Lei, Y. (2019). A developmental history of forensic speaker comparison in the UK. *Evidence Science, 27*, (6): 730–740.

Fillmore, C. J. (1968). The case for case. In E. Bach & R. Harms (eds.), *Universals in Linguistic Theory* (pp. 1–88). New York: Holt, Rinehart & Winston.

Gales, T. (2010). Ideologies of violence: A corpus and discourse analytic approach to stance in threatening communications. *International Journal of Speech Language and the Law, 17*(2): 299–302.

Gales, T. (2011). Identifying interpersonal stance in threatening discourse: An appraisal analysis. *Discourse Studies, 13*(1): 27–46.

Gales, T. (2015). Threatening Stances: A corpus analysis of realized vs. non-realized threats. *Language and Law / Linguagem e Direito, 2*(2): 1–25.

Gales, T. & Solan, L. (2017). Witness cross-examinations in non-stranger assault crimes: An appraisal analysis. *Language and Law / Linguagem e Direito, 4*(2): 108–139.

Ge, Y. (2013). *Solicitation of Desired Information in Courtroom Questioning: A Discourse Information Processing Perspective*. Jinan: Shandong University Press.

Ge, Y. (2018). *Resolution of Conflict of Interest in Chinese Civil Court Hearings: A Perspective of Discourse Information Theory.* New York: Peter Lang.

Gibbons, J. (2003). *Forensic Linguistics: An Introduction to Language in the Justice System.* Britain: Blackwell.

Gluzman, H. (2018). Back to the future: Reviving the use of video link evidence in Canadian criminal courts. *Canadian Journal of Law and Technology,* *16*(1): 183–193.

Grant, T. (2021). Txt 4n6: Idiolect free authorship analysis? In M. Coulthard, A. May & R. Sousa-Silva (eds.), *The Routledge Handbook of Forensic Linguistics* (pp. 558–575). Oxon: Routledge.

Grant, T. (2022). *The Idea of Progress in Forensic Authorship Analysis: Elements in Forensic Linguistics.* Cambridge: Cambridge University Press.

Guo, J. (2023). *Awakening Justifiable Defence: The Study of Evaluation in Media Reports on Self-defence Cases.* Unpublished PhD thesis, Guangdong University of Foreign Studies.

Guo, W. (2022). *Information Processing in the Summing Up of Issues in Chinese Civil Court Hearings: A Discourse Information Perspective.* MA thesis, Guangdong University of Foreign Studies.

Halliday, M. A. K. (1985/1994). *An Introduction to Functional Grammar.* London: Edward Arnold.

He, X. (2021). The nature of persons with expertise and their effectiveness in the law of evidence. *Minutes of the 31st Judges' Meeting of 2019.* The Second Circuit Court of the Supreme Court.

Heffer, C. (2007). Judgement in court: Evaluating participants in courtroom discourse. In K. Kredens & S. Gozdz-Roszkowski (eds.), *Language and the Law: International Outlooks* (pp. 145–179). Frankfurt am Mein: Perter Lang GmbH.

Hibbitts, B. J. (1994). Making sense of metaphors: Visuality, aurality, and the reconfiguration of American legal discourse. *Cardozo Law Review*, 16: 229–356.

Hinduja, S. & Patchin, J. W. (2008). Cyberbullying: An exploratory analysis of factors related to offending and victimization. *Deviant Behavior*, *29*(2): 129–156.

Hu, Z. (1994). *Cohesion and Coherence in Discourse.* Shanghai: Shanghai Foreign Language Education Press.

Huai, Y. (2021). *Multimodal Discourse Information Processing in English Classroom Instruction for Legal Purposes.* Ohio: American Academic Press.

Huang, H. (2021). *Information Processing in the Compilation of Chinese Guiding Cases: From the Perspective of Discourse Information*. MA thesis, Guangdong University of Foreign Studies.

Huang, P. & Wang, T. (2013). Interpretation and application of the pragmatic goal principle. *Heilongjiang Social Sciences, 139*(4): 128–130.

Hunter, M. & Grant, T. (2022). Killer stance: An investigation of the relationship between attitudinal resources and psychological traits in the writings of four serial murderers. *Language and Law / Linguagem e Direito, 9*(1): 48–72.

Hurt, M. (2020). *Pledging to Harm: A Linguistic Analysis of Violent Intent in Threatening Language*. Unpublished PhD thesis, Aston University.

Hurt, M. & Grant, T. (2019). Pledging to harm: A linguistics appraisal analysis of judgement comparing realized and non-realized violent fantasies. *Discourse & Society, 30*(2): 154–171.

Ira-Katharina, P. & Petermann, F. (2018). Cyberbullying: A concept analysis of defining attributes and additional influencing factors. *Computers in Human Behavior, 86*: 350–366.

Jacobs, T. A. (2020). *Cyberbullying law*. Chicago: American Bar Association.

Jessen, M., Cao, H. & Wang, Y. (2010). Forensic Phonetics. *Evidence Science, 17*(5): 712–738.

Jiang, J. (1990). On the expressive coloration of legal language. *Journal of Shanghai University of Political Science and Law (The Rule of Law Forum), 5*(3): 42–45,49.

Jiang, J. (1994). Contextual composition of legal speech. *Journal of Shanghai University of Political Science and Law (The Rule of Law Forum), 9*(5): 60–62.

Jiang, J. (1995). *Legal Language and Speech Research*. Beijing: Mass Publishing House.

Jing, H. (2022). Innovation and contributions of China's internet courts. *China Legal Science, 39*(4): 49–73.

Jones, A. (1994). The limitations of voice identification. In J. Gibbons (ed.), *Language and Law* (pp. 346–362). Harlow: Longman.

Klomek, A. B., Sourander, A. & Gould, M. (2010). The association of suicide and bullying in childhood to young adulthood: A review of cross-sectional and longitudinal research findings. *The Canadian Journal of Psychiatry, 55*(5): 282–288.

Körner, H. (2000). *Negotiating Authority: The Logogenesis of Dialogue in Common Law Judgments*. Unpublished PhD Dissertation, University of Sydney, NSW.

Labov, W. & Fanshel, D. (1977). *Therapeutic Discourse: Psychotherapy As Conversation*. New York: Academic Press.

Lasswell, H. D. (1948). The structure and function of communication in society. In Bryson, L. (ed.), *The Communication of Ideas* (pp. 37–51). New York: Harper & Row.

Levi, J. N. & Walker, A. G. (1990). *Language in the Judicial Process*. New York: Plenum Press.

Li, K. (2010). On static equivalence in translating legal texts. *Foreign Language Teaching and Research*, 42(1)1: 59–65,81.

Li, K. & Zhang, X. (2005). *Legal Texts and Legal Ttranslation*. Beijing: China Translation Corporation.

Li, W. & Wang, Z. (2019). A multimodal study of forensic linguistics: Current research and prospects. *Journal of SJTU (Philosophy and Social Sciences)*, 27(5): 110–119.

Liao, M. (2002). The status quo of Chinese courtroom trials from linguistic perspective. *Applied Linguistics*, 11(4): 25–36.

Liao, M. (2003). *Courtroom Questions, Responses and their Interaction*. Beijing: Law Press.

Liao, M. (2004a). A review of study of forensic linguistics abroad. *Contemporary Rhetoric*, 43(1): 66–76,94.

Liao, M. (2004b). A study on the principle of goal and cooperation in the courtroom interactive discourse. *Foreign Language Research*, 43(5): 43–52.

Liao, M. (2005a). The 'principle of goal' and goal analysis (I): Exploring new approaches to pragmatic research. *Contemporary Rhetoric*, 44(3): 1–10.

Liao, M. (2005b). The 'principle of Goal' and goal analysis (II): A new approach to pragmatic discourse analysis. *Contemporary Rhetoric*, 44(4): 5–11.

Liao, M. (2005c). The principle of goal and analysis of discourse coherence: A new approach to the study of discourse coherence. *Foreign Language Teaching and Research*, 49(5): 351–357.

Liao, M. (2004, 2005, 2009). *Trial Communication Strategies*. Beijing: Law Press.

Liao, M. (2006). A study on 'formulation' in Chinese courtroom interaction. *Foreign Languages Research*, 23(2): 1–8,13,80.

Liao, M. (2007). Pragmatics and jurisprudence: Application of the principle of cooperation in legislative communication. *Journal of Comparative Law*, 21(5): 45–63.

Liao, M. (2009a). The principle of goal direction and goal analysis. *Foreign Language Research*, 32(4): 62–64.

Liao, M. (2009b). The principle of goal direction and goal analysis (Continued). *Foreign Language Research*, 32(6): 101–109.

Liao, M. (2009c). A study of interruption in Chinese criminal courtroom discourse. *Text & Talk, 29*(2): 175–199.

Liao, M. (2010). The principle of goal and dynamics of context. *Journal of PLA University of Foreign Languages, 33*(4): 1–5,127.

Liao, M. (2012a). The principle of goal direction and interaction of speech acts. *Foreign Language Research, 35*(5): 23–30.

Liao, M. (2012b). Courtroom discourse in China. In P. Tiersma & L. M. Solan (eds.), *The Oxford Handbook of Language and Law* (pp. 395–407). Oxford: Oxford University Press.

Liao, M. (2013a). The principle of goal and contextual studies: On human beings as the key factor of the context. *Foreign Language Education & Research, 1*(1): 17–21.

Liao, M. (2013b). Power in interruption. In W. Christopher & G. Tessuto (eds.), *Language in the Negotiation of Justice: Contexts, Issues and Applications* (pp. 33–48). Surrey, UK: Ashgate Publishing Group.

Liao, M. (2015). Speech or silence: Within & beyond language and law. In M. L. Solan, J. Ainsworth & R. Shuy (eds.), *Speaking of Language and Law: Conversation on the Work of Peter Tiersma* (pp. 164-185). Oxford: Oxford University Press.

Liao, M. & Gong, J. (2015). Interruption in courtroom discourse and gender differences. *Contemporary Rhetoric, 34*(1):43–55.

Lin, K. & Ji, M. (2002). Discussion on the translation of the ' de' structure in legal texts. *Shanghai Journal of Translators, 3*: 20–22.

Liu, M. & Han, H. (2016). Litigation status, evidentiary effect and scope of cross-examination of 'persons with expertise' in criminal proceedings. *Journal of CUPL (China University of Political Science and Law), 52*(2): 100–106.

Liu, M. (2019). Improvement of the system of participation of 'persons with expertise' in criminal proceedings. *Law-Based Society, 4*(4): 102–109.

Liu, W. (2009). Forensic linguistics research in evidence. *Journal of Guangdong University of Foreign Studies, 20*(1): 68–72.

Liu, X. & Wang, Y. (2014). Study on the expert assistant qualification review. *Evidence Science, 21*(6): 698–715.

Liu, Y. (2019a). *Multimodal Construction of 'Rule of Law' in Chinese Anti-corruption Public Service Advertisements: A Social Semiotic Approach.* Unpublished PhD thesis, Guangdong University of Foreign Studies.

Liu, Y. (2019b). Multimodal construction of 'rule of law' in Chinese anti-corruption public service advertisements: A social semiotic approach

(PhD abstract). *The International Journal of Speech, Language and the Law, 26*(2): 287–290.

Liu, Y. & Yuan, C. (2022). Multimodal construction of the 'Rule of Law': A genre analysis of anticorruption public service advertisements. *Journal of Beijing International Studies University, 44*(2): 51–65.

Lou, K. (2007). On role of linguistics and communication in analysis and attestation of verbal evidence: Taking Yang's prosecution against Hu on infringement of right of reputation as an example. *Evidence Science, 15* (1,2): 78–83.

Lu, J. (2000). A distinctive monograph on legal language research – reading Wang Jie's Legal Language Research. *Applied Linguistics, 9*(3): 110–112.

Lu, N. (2021). *The Discursive Construction of Legal Reasoning: A Genre Study of the United States Supreme Court.* Unpublished PhD thesis, Guangdong University of Foreign Studies.

Lu, N. & Yuan, C. (2021). Legal reasoning: A textual perspective on common law judicial opinions and Chinese judgments. *Text & Talk, 41*(1): 71–93.

Lu, N. & Yuan, C. (2022). Judicial opinions as a genre simplex with an embedding structure. *Journal of Foreign Languages, 23*(3): 34–47.

Luchjenbroers, J. (1997). In your own words: Questions and answers in a Supreme Court trial. *Journal of Pragmatics 27(4)*: 477–503.

Luo, H. (2012). A Preliminary study on author identification: Combined with DIA theory analysis. *Journal of Language and Literature Studies 32*(10): 16–18,20.

Luo, X. (2023). *Tenor Negotiation in Community Correction Discourse: A Judicial Practice Navigating between Retributive Justice and Restorative Justice.* Unpublished PhD thesis, Guangdong University of Foreign Studies.

Luo, X. & Yuan, C. (2019). An analysis of preliminary assessment discourse of community correction: From the perspective of genre structure and exchange structure. *Journal of Guangdong University of Foreign Studies, 30*(3): 39–47.

Ma, Q. (2017). The status quo of MTI education and countermeasures at Universities of Political Science & Law in China. *Chinese Translators Journal, 14*(4): 21–27.

Martin, J. R. & Zappavigna, M. (2016). Exploring restorative justice: Dialectics of theory and practice. *International Journal of Speech Language and the Law, 23*(2): 215–242.

Martin, J. R. & Zappavigna, M. (2019). Embodied meaning: A systemic functional perspective on paralanguage. *Functional Linguistics, 6*(1): 1–33.

Martin, J. R., Zappavigna, M. & Dwyer, P. (2012). Beyond redemption: Choice and consequence in youth justice conferencing. In J. R. Martin & Z. Wang (eds.), *Forensic Linguistics* (pp. 227–258). Shanghai: Shanghai Jiao Tong University Press.

Martin, J. R., Zappavigna, M., Dwyer, P. & Cléirigh, C. (2013). Users in uses of language: Embodied identity in youth justice conferencing. *Text & Talk, 33* (4–5): 467–496.

Mathesius, V. (1929). Zur Satzperspektive im modernen English. *Archiv flir das Studium der modern Sprachen und Literaruren, 155*: 200–210.

Matoesian, G. M. (1993). *Reproducing Rape: Domination through Talk in the Courtroom*. Chicago: University of Chicago Press.

McMenamin, G. (2021). The theory and practice of forensic stylistics. In M. Coulthard, A. May & R. Sousa- Silva (eds.), *The Routledge Handbook of Forensic Linguistics* (pp. 539–557). Oxon: Routledge.

Mellinkoff, D. (1963). *The Language of the Law*. Boston: Little, Brown and Company.

Miller & Kimberly (2017). Cyberbullying and its consequences: How cyber-bullying is contorting the minds of victims and bullies alike, and the law's limited available redress. *Southern California Interdisciplinary Law Journal, 26*(2): 379–404.

Nini, A. & Grant, T. (2013). Bridging the gap between stylistic and cognitive approaches to authorship analysis using systemic functional linguistics and multidimensional analysis. *International Journal of Speech, Language & the Law, 20*(2): 173–202.

O'Barr, W. (1982). *Linguistic Evidence: Language, Power and Strategy in the Courtroom*. New York: Academic Press.

Pan, Q. (1983). Several Issues on Legal Style. Weekly Newspaper of East China College of Political Science and Law. July 7.

Pan, Q. (1987). Objects, scope and methodology of legal stylistics. *Zhongzhou Journal, 9*(1): 95–96.

Pan, Q. (1989). *The Art of Legal Language*. Shanghai: Xue Lin Publishing House.

Pan, Q. (1991). *Exploration of Legal Language Styles*. Kunming: Yunnan People's Publishing House.

Pan, Q. (1997). *Chinese Legal Language in the Cross-Century*. Wuhan: East China University of Science and Technology Press.

Pan, Q. (2004). *Chinese Legal Language Assessment*. Anhui: Chinese Dictionary.

Pan, Q. (2015). Language Rights Comprehensive Protection of Juvenile Criminal Defendants in the Context of Rule-by-Law. Conference paper at the *12th Biennial Conference of the International Association for Forensic*

Linguists (IAFL 12), Guangzhou, China in 2015, www.flrchina.com/001/108.html.

Pan, Q. (2017). *Forensic Linguistics*. Beijing: China University of Political Science & Law Press.

Pan, Q. (2019a). A comparative examination of the past and present Chinese and English legal languages and their reform and optimization. *Language Weekly*, 2019–11–2, 2019–1–9.

Pan, Q. (2019b). The language dilemma of the 'valley people' facing the Law. *Language Weekly*, 2019–11–6, 2019–11–13.

Pan, Q. (2019c). The legal embarrassment and language problems faced by vulnerable groups: Taking the poor educated or people of low social and economic status as examples. *Language and Law Studies*, *1*(1): 24–39.

Pan, X. & Du, J. (2011). Information flow of process control in courtroom question and response. *Journal of Foreign Languages*, *34*(2): 56–63.

Posner, R. (2013). *Reflections on Judging*. Cambridge, MA: Harvard University Press.

Prince, E. F. (1981). Toward a taxonomy of given-new information. In P. Cole (ed.), *Syntax and Semantics: Vol. 14. Radical Pragmatics* (pp. 223–255). New York: Academic Press.

Qiu, D. (1980). The application of linguistic analysis in detecting and solving crimes. *Forensic Science and Technology*, *5*(5): 27–32.

Qiu, D. (1981). How to analyse speech in cases. *Forensic Science and Technology*, *6*(2):31–38.

Qiu, D. (1985). *Speech Recognition*. Beijing: Mass Publishing House.

Qiu, D. (1991). The origin and development of investigative linguistics in China. *Language Planning*, *36*(6): 37–38.

Qiu, D. (1995). *Investigative Linguistics*. Beijing: China People's Public Security University Press.

Qu, T. & Wang, Z. (2022). Modelling multimodal design in conflict negotiation discourse. *Modern Foreign Languages*, *45*(6): 780–793.

Qu, W. (2012). Reflections on the problems and their causes of the translation of Chinese legal terms. *Chinese Translators Journal*, 33(6) 68–75.

Qu, W. (2022). The system of principles of foreign translation of Chinese legislative texts: Based on the English translation practice of Chinese Civil Laws. *Foreign Languages in China*, 19(1): 1, 10–20.

Ramos, P. (2021). Translating legal terminology and phraseology: between inter-systemic incongruity and multilingual harmonization. *Perspectives*, *29*(2): 175–183.

Roberts, C. (1996). Information structure in discourse: Towards an integrated formal theory of pragmatics. *OSU Working Papers in Linguistics, 49*: 91–136.

Sampasa-Kanyinga, H., Roumeliotis, P. & Xu, H. (2014). Associations between cyberbullying and school bullying victimization and suicidal ideation, plans and attempts among Canadian schoolchildren. *PloS One, 9*(7): e102145.

Sarcevic, S. (1997). *New Approach to Legal Translation*. The Hague: Kluwer Law International.

Shuy, R. (1993). *Language Crimes: The Use and Abuse of Language Evidence in the Courtroom*. Cambridge, MA: Blackwell Publishers.

Shuy, R. W. (1987). *The Language of Confession, Interrogation and Deception*. Thousand Oaks CA: Sage.

Smith, P. K., Mahdavi, J., Carvalho, M., et al. (2008). Cyberbullying: Its nature and impact in secondary school pupils. *Journal of Child Psychology and Psychiatry, and Allied Disciplines, 49*(4): 376–385.

Song, D. & Wan, Y. (2021). The role of 'persons with expertise' in criminal proceedings. *Journal of Sichuan Police College,-33*(6):14–23.

Stygall, G. (1994). *Trial Language: Differential Discourse Processing and Discursive Formation*. Philadelphia, PA: John Benjamins.

Su, B. (2022). Construction of criminal expert assistant (legal) aid assistance system. *Evidence Science, 29*(5): 587–599.

Su, L. (2023). Thinking about things, not words – a fragment of thought on 'legal language'. *Oriental Jurisprudence, 16*(1): 91–101.

Sun, Y. & Zhou, G. (1997). *Legal Linguistics*. Beijing: China University of Political Science and Law Press.

Sung, H.-C. (2020). Can online courts promote access to justice? A case study of the internet courts in China. *The Computer Law and Security Report, 39*: 105461.

Tao, J. (2018). *From Guilt to Innocence: Discursive Construction of the Presumption of Innocence in Legal News Discourse*. Unpublished PhD thesis, Guangdong University of Foreign Studies.

Tiersma, P. (1999). *Legal Language*. Chicago: University of Chicago Press.

Tiersma, P. (2005). Some myths about legal language. *Legal Studies Paper No. 2005–26*, Loyola Law School. http://ssrn.com/abstract=845928.

Tian, H. & Wang, Z. (2016). Distributional features of attitudinal resources in statements of defense in Chinese criminal trials: Legal discourse as social process. *Shandong Foreign Language Teaching, 37*(2): 13–21.

Tian, J. (2008). *Courtroom Interpreters' Decision Making in Information Processing*. MA thesis, Guangdong University of Foreign Studies.

van Dijk, T. A. & Kintsch, W. (1983). *Strategies of Discourse Comprehension*. New York: Academic Press.

van Dijk, T. A. (2008). *Discourse and Context: A Socio-cognitive Approach.* Cambridge: Cambridge University Press.

Walsh, M. (1994). Interactional Styles in the courtroom. In J. Gibbons (ed.), *Language and Law* (pp. 217–233). Harlow: Longman.

Wang, J. (1996). The intersection of linguistics and jurisprudence—an introduction to the Legal Linguistics Coursebook. *Applied Linguistics, 5*(4): 90–94.

Wang, J. (1997). *Legal Linguistics Coursebook.* Beijing: Law Press.

Wang, J. (1999). *Legal Language Research.* Guangzhou: Guangdong Education Press.

Wang, J. (2004). Exploring the interactive language in prosecution and defense court trials. *Applied Linguistics, 13*(3): 76–82.

Wang, J. (2010). Research on legal language in mainland China from the 'legislative era' to the 'law revision era'. *Applied Linguistics, 19*(4): 2–9.

Wang, J. (2011). Analysis and authentication of linguistic evidence and its judicial application. *Contemporary Rhetoric, 30*(2): 27–31.

Wang, J., Su, J. Z., & Joseph G. Toury, eds. (2006). *Law-Language-Linguistic Diversity: Proceedings of the Ninth International Symposium on Law and Language.* Beijing: Law Press.

Wang, P. & Wang, Z. (2016). A study on the legal discourse and ideational meaning of social processes – Taking the marriage law of the people's republic of China as an example. *Contemporary Rhetoric, 35*(4): 56–67.

Wang, S. (2023). *A Genre Study of Police Interrogation Discourse: From Investigation Centeredness to Trial Centeredness.* Unpublished PhD thesis, Guangdong University of Foreign Studies.

Wang, Y., Li, J. & Cao, H. (2012). An overview of voiceprint identification studies. *Police Technology, 28*(4): 54–56.

Wang, Z. (2001). Appraisal systems and their operation: A new development in the systemic functional linguistics. *Journal of Foreign Languages, 24*(6): 13–20.

Wang, Z. & Liu, C. (2014). Attitudinal bonding in construing interpersonal harmony. *Foreign Languages in China, 11*(3): 19–25,33.

Wang, Z. & Tian, H. (2017). Legal discourse as a social process: From the SFL-based discourse semantics perspective. *Linguistic Research, 38*(1): 199–212.

Wang, Z. & Zhang, Q. (2015). Legal discourse as a social process and its textual semantics. *Foreign Language Teaching, 59*(1): 1–6.

Wei, Y. (2008). On burden of proof for ambiguous facts in reputation right cases. *Chinese Journal of Journalism & Communication, 48*(2): 5–10.

Wu, W. (1994). Forensic linguistics: Conferences, institutions and journals. *Linguistics Abroad, 33*(2): 44–50.

Wu, W. (1995). Chinese evidence versus the institutionalized power of English. *Forensic Linguistics*, *2*(2): 154–167.

Wu, W. (2002a). Formation, status and classification of forensic linguistics abroad. *New Horizons in the Study of Language and Law–Proceedings of the First Symposium on Language and Law*. (pp. 157–173). Beijing: Chinese Society for Ethnolinguistics.

Wu, W. (2002b). Forensic linguistics: Data-based research methods. *Contemporary Linguistics*, *41*(1): 38–45,78.

Wu, W. (2002c). *Language and the Law: Linguistic Research in the Legal Field*. Shanghai: Shanghai Foreign Language Education Press.

Xiong, Y. (2016). *Authorship Identification of Anonymous Report Letters: From the Perspective of DIT*. MA thesis, Guangdong University of Foreign Studies.

Xu, D. (2017). Dilemma and countermeasures on cultivation of MLTI legal translation talents. *Foreign Languages in China*, *14*(4): 14–20.

Xu, Y. (2013). *Realization of Persuasion in Chinese Court Conciliation: The Discourse Information Approach*. Beijing: Science Press.

Xu, Y. (2014). Realisation of persuasion in Chinese court conciliation: A discourse information perspective (doctoral thesis abstract). *International Journal of Speech, Language and the Law*, *21*(1): 157–162.

Xu, Y. (2016). A new breakthrough in the theoretical construction of legal linguistics: A review of legal discourse information. *Journal of Zhongyuan University of Technology*, *27*(2): 36–40.

Xu, Y. (2020). The invisible aggressive fist: Features of cyberbullying language in China. *International Journal for the Semiotics of Law*, *33*(34): 1041–1064.

Xu, Y. (2021). Every Little Bit Counts: Identifying Implicit Cyberbullying Language on the Chinese Social Media. Conference paper presented at the *Fifteenth Conference of the International Association of Forensic Linguists*, September 13–16. Birmingham: the University of Aston.

Xu, Y. (2024). *Semiotic (De)construction of Judges' Identities in China's Internet Courts*. Cheltenham: Edward Elgar. In Press.

Xu, Y. & Trzaskawka, P. (2021). Towards descriptive adequacy of cyberbullying: Interdisciplinary studies on features, cases and legislative concerns of cyberbullying. *International Journal for the Semiotics of Law*, *34*(4): 929–943.

Xu, Y. & Yu, W. (2023). Legal translation and interpreting in China: Practices, theoretical studies and future trends. In A. Wagner & A. Matulewska (eds.), *Research Handbook on Lurilinguistics* (pp. 418–435). Cheltenham: Edward Elgar Publishing Ltd.

Yuan, C. (2008). Interpersonal meanings in police interrogations: An appraisal-engagement perspective. *Modern Foreign Languages, 31*(2): 141–149.

Yuan, C. (2010). *Avoiding Revictimization: A Study of Police Interrogation Speech*. Beijing: Foreign Language Teaching and Research Press.

Yuan, C. & Liao, Z. (2010). The covert persuasiveness of rhetoric questions in lawyers' defense speeches: Attitude perspective. *Contemporary Rhetoric, 29*(4): 24–30.

Yuan, C. & Hu, J. (2011). An adaptation analysis of engagement resources in lawyer representation. *Language Teaching and Linguistic Studies, 33*(3): 87–94.

Yuan, C. & Hu, J. (2012). Punishing Crimes: An analysis of appraisal resources in public prosecution's statements. *Journal of Guangdong University of Foreign Studies, 23*(3): 55–59.

Yuan, C., Zhang, S. & He, Q. (2018). Popularity of Latin and law French in legal English: A corpus-based disciplinary study of the language of the law. *Linguistics and Human Sciences. 14*(1–2): 151–174.

Yuan, C. & Luo, X. (2021). A negotiation analysis of risk assessment in community correction from the perspective of exchange structure. *Language and Dialogue, 11*(2): 200–222.

Yuan, C., Cao, H. & Zheng, J. (2023). Multimodal attitude analysis of Attorneys' closing arguments and narrative construction. *Modern Foreign Languages, 46*(3): 319–331.

Yuan, C., He, Y. & Liu, Y. (2021). Rule by law versus rule of law: A multimodal analysis of persuasion and legal ideologies in anti-corruption discourse in China. *Multimodality & Society, 1*(4): 429–454.

Yuan, C., Xu, Y. & Zhang, S. (2024). *Forensic and Legal Linguistics: New Perspectives and Development*. Beijing: Tsinghua University Press.

Zappavinga, M. & Martin, J. R. 2018. *Discourse and Diversionary Justice: An Analysis of Youth Justice Conferencing*. New York: Palgrave Macmillan.

Zhang, C. & Zhuo, Y. (2020). Expert Assistant System: Expert Witness in China? – Guide to China's Civil Evidence Rules (13). *China Justice Observer*.(www.chinajusticeobserver.com/a/expert-assistant-system-expert-witness-in-china-guide-to-chinas-civil-evidence-rules-13).

Zhang, F. (2018). A study on legal translation teaching and talents cultivation in the context of 'One Belt, One Road'. *Chinese Translators Journal, 40*(2): 31–35.

Zhang, F. (2021). On the construction of quality assessment of legal translation: Taking the English translation of the Civil Code of the People's Republic of China as a case. *Chinese Translators Journal, 43*(5): 121–130.

Zhang, L. (2011). *Lawyer Evaluation in Chinese Courtroom*. Beijing: Knowledge.

Zhang, L. & Wang, Z. (2022). A study of the normalization of expert opinion based on linguistic evidence. *Chinese Journal of Forensic Sciences, 23*(1): 100–104.

Zhang, Q. (2010). An Analysis of the Purpose Relations in the Courtroom Discourse. *Journal of Shanxi University (Philosophy and Social Science), 33*(6): 130–133.

Zhang, S. (2020). The application of idiolect features to authorship attribution for Chinese short texts. *Chinese Journal of Forensic Sciences, 21*(2): 56–63.

Zhang, S. (2021). From flaming to incited crime: Recognising cyberbullying on Chinese WeChat account. *International Journal for the Semiotics of Law, 34*(4): 1093–1116.

Zhang, X. (2001). Text type and legal texts. *Modern Foreign Languages, 24*(2): 192–200.

Zhang, Y. (2007). Textual interpretation of linguistic evidence. *Contemporary Rhetoric* (formerly *Rhetorical Studies*), *26*(6): 25–27,40.

Zhang, S. (2016). A study on authorship attribution of Chinese texts based on discourse information analysis. *International Journal of Speech, Language and the Law, 23*(1): 147–150.

Zhao, H. & Wang, Z. (2022). Intermodal construction of lawyer identity: Interaction between linguistic and non-linguistic signs. Modern Foreign Languages, *45*(5): 597–610.

Zhao, J. (2011). *A Chinese-English Contrastive Discourse Analysis: On the Information Structure and Its Linguistic Realizations in Legal Discourse*. Beijing: Science Press.

Zhao, J. (2018). On the disciplinary construction of legal translation in MTI education: Notions and pedagogical implications. *Foreign Language and Literature Studies, 35*(2): 192–202.

Zhao, J. & Xue, J. (2022). Conceptual transplantation and equivalent interpretation in legal translation: Translating key terms of the Civil Code of the People's Republic of China. *Shanghai Journal of Translators, 37*(1): 27–33.

Zhao, J. & Xue, J. (2023). Translation strategies for rule-of-law terms with Chinese characteristics in the new era: Standardization and communication. *Shanghai Journal of Translators, 38*(1): 24–30,96.

Zheng, J. (2019a). *A Study of Psycho-correction Discourse in Community Correction Under Restorative Justice from the Perspective of Individuation*. Unpublished PhD thesis, Guangdong University of Foreign Studies.

Zheng, J. (2019b). An individuation study of identity construction via multi-modal discourse in community corrections. *Journal of Xi'an International Studies University, 27*(2): 37–42.

Zheng, J. & Yuan, C. (2018). Multimodal discourse construction of the defendant's identity in community correction pre-trial social investigation and evaluation. *Journal of Political Science and Law, 35*(4): 62–69.

Zheng, J. & Yuan, C. (2021). Discursive construction of identities of judicial social workers in community correction. *Modern Foreign Languages, 44*(2): 183–195.

Zheng, X. & Wang, Y. (2021, September 13–15). *Changed space and reconstructed meaning a semiotic analysis of the Internet courthouse in China.* 15th Biennial Conference of the International Association of Forensic Linguists, Aston University.

Zhou, Q. (2017). Strengthening the construction of Hangzhou Internet Court, exploring new modes of cyber justice and serving the building of a strong internet country. *China Journal of Applied Jurisprudence, 1*(5): 1–4.

Zou, Y. (2008). Types of linguistic evidence and their semantic examination. *Journal of China University of Political Science and Law, 2*(3): 96–102.

Zou, Y. (2018). Is legal linguistics 'the language of the law' or 'linguistics of the law' or 'law and language': Also on the discipline connotation and orientation of legal linguistics. *Journal of Liaoning Normal University (Social Science), 41*(1): 8–12.

Acknowledgements

This Element is the result of close collaboration among the three authors, who are colleagues at the Guangdong University of Foreign Studies (GDUFS), the leading institute of forensic linguistics in China and the venue of IAFL12 in 2015. It is also the result of frequent communications with the pioneering figures within the CAFL, such as distinguished professors Pan Qingyun, Wangjie, Du Jinbang, and Wang Zhenhua, to name a few, who contributed good ideas and suggestions in writing this book.

We are grateful to Tim Grant and Tammy Gales, the editors of this Elements series, for their interest in China's forensic linguistics and their trust in the authors' capacity in writing this Element. Our sincere thanks also go to the anonymous reviewers who gave positive comments and valuable suggestions on revising the manuscript.

We'd like to offer special thanks to Dr Terry Royce, a distinguished Australian forensic linguist at the University of Technology, Sydney (UTS) who serves as a Yunshan Scholar at GDUFS, a prestigious position held by renowned professors worldwide. Apart from lecturing, Terry is of great help in developing the research profile of the Forensic Linguistics faculty at GDUFS. He has been enthusiastically engaged in discussing the topics in this Element and revising the manuscript according to the reviewers' comments.

Finally, we'd like to acknowledge the research funding offered by the research project granted by the Ministry of Education 'Identification of Linguistic Patterns in Cyberbullying on China's Main Social Media Platforms' (22YJC740089).

Cambridge Elements ≡

Forensic Linguistics

Tim Grant

Aston University

Tim Grant is Professor of Forensic Linguistics, Director of the Aston Institute for Forensic Linguistics, and past president of the International Association of Forensic Linguists. His recent publications have focussed on online sexual abuse conversations including *Language and Online Identities: The Undercover Policing of Internet Sexual Crime* (with Nicci MacLeod, Cambridge, 2020).

Tim is one of the world's most experienced forensic linguistic practitioners and his case work has involved the analysis of abusive and threatening communications in many different contexts including investigations into sexual assault, stalking, murder, and terrorism. He also makes regular media contributions including presenting police appeals such as for the BBC Crimewatch programme.

Tammy Gales

Hofstra University

Tammy Gales is an Associate Professor of Linguistics and the Director of Research at the Institute for Forensic Linguistics, Threat Assessment, and Strategic Analysis at Hofstra University, New York. She has served on the Executive Committee for the International Association of Forensic Linguists (IAFL), is on the editorial board for the peer-reviewed journals Applied Corpus Linguistics and Language and Law / Linguagem e Direito, and is a member of the advisory board for the BYU Law and Corpus Linguistics group. Her research interests cross the boundaries of forensic linguistics and language and the law, with a primary focus on threatening communications. She has trained law enforcement agents from agencies across Canada and the U.S. and has applied her work to both criminal and civil cases.

About the Series

Elements in Forensic Linguistics provides high-quality accessible writing, bringing cutting-edge forensic linguistics to students and researchers as well as to practitioners in law enforcement and law. Elements in the series range from descriptive linguistics work, documenting a full range of legal and forensic texts and contexts; empirical findings and methodological developments to enhance research, investigative advice, and evidence for courts; and explorations into the theoretical and ethical foundations of research and practice in forensic linguistics.

Cambridge Elements ☰

Forensic Linguistics

Elements in the Series

A full series listing is available at: www.cambridge.org/EIFL

Printed in the United States
by Baker & Taylor Publisher Services